To Mary, Lloy[d]
thank you fo[r]
blessings of your
hospitality — happy
thanksgiving!
Love, Kathy, Walt,
Shannon & Nick

D0498678

## Praise for
### *Potluck*

"Always the gifted observer, Kim Thomas has given us a feast in *Potluck,* a book that creatively melds sage wisdom with recipes. Laugh-out-loud funny and brilliantly written, this book celebrates and affirms community. A delightful and fresh offering as original as Kim herself."

—MARGARET BECKER, artist, author, speaker

"Kim Thomas's way with a pen is as delicious as the potlucks she writes about. With elegant prose, she gently invites us to contemplate the sacrament of sharing a meal together, whether with family, friends, or our faith communities. Her stories will kindle your own memories of potlucks and remind you of how those experiences shaped your life. Even if you didn't grow up with the potluck tradition, there's still a place for you at the table. This culinary memoir is pure soul food."

—CINDY CROSBY, author of *By Willoway Brook*
and *Waiting for Morning*

"Kim Thomas's new book *Potluck* makes me hungry. I'm hungry for the preparation, service, and messiness of relating to people deeply. Kim's life makes me hungry. I'm hungry for the existence she has carved out for herself, one of beauty and truth and faith. Once again Kim shows by example what loving people looks like, around the table and around the corners of God's community, and she invites us all to join the party of belonging."

> —JUDY NELSON, editor in chief of *Worldwide Challenge* magazine, Campus Crusade for Christ

"Deep in the soul of every man and woman is the desire to belong, to be noticed. Kim Thomas poignantly illustrates this universal need through real-life situations, and her style is as inviting and succulent as the recipes she includes. Come on in."

> —DAVID DURHAM, founder and executive director of The Crucible International

"What a delightful book! I don't cook, but I just might try some of these recipes and rejoice as I think of the stories that make food more than 'just food.' Authentic, encouraging, and profound. You'll love this book."

> —STEVE BROWN, professor at Reformed Theological Seminary, author of *A Scandalous Freedom,* and teacher on *Key Life* radio program

"If you have ever been to a potluck, or if you have never been to a potluck, or if (bless your heart) you do not know what a potluck is, read this book. It is beautiful and heartbreaking and honest and true."

> —ROBERT BENSON, author of *Home by Another Way*

# POTLUCK

# POTLUCK

*Parables of Giving, Taking, and Belonging*

# KIM THOMAS

WaterBrook
PRESS

POTLUCK
PUBLISHED BY WATERBROOK PRESS
12265 Oracle Boulevard, Suite 200
Colorado Springs, Colorado 80921
*A division of Random House, Inc.*

All Scripture quotations, unless otherwise indicated, are taken from the
New American Standard Bible®. © Copyright The Lockman Foundation
1960, 1962, 1963, 1968, 1971, 1972, 1973, 1975, 1977, 1995. Used by
permission. (www.Lockman.org).

ISBN 1-4000-7118-6

Details in some anecdotes and stories have been changed to protect the
identities of the persons involved.

Library of Congress Cataloging-in-Publication Data
Thomas, Kim, 1958–
  Potluck : parables of giving, taking, and belonging / Kim Thomas.—1st ed.
     p. cm.
  Includes bibliographical references and index.
  ISBN 1-4000-7118-6
  1. Community—Religious aspects—Christianity.  2. Cookery—Religious
aspects—Christianity. I. Title.
  BV625.T46  2006
  242—dc22

                                                    2005035504

Printed in the United States of America
2006—First Edition

10  9  8  7  6  5  4  3  2  1

*For Sara and Robert—*
*At the potluck lunch we shared in your backyard*
*under the maple, you gave me the confidence to tell*
*this story. You continually remind me why I love*
*writing and words. You also remind me how big the*
*potluck table is and that there are a lot of chairs.*
*Jim will sit in the one on the right; Robert, the one*
*on the left. Sara and I will sit on the swing.*

# Contents

# First Memories

## *The Community of Family*

Southern women with the soft beauty of a flower and the resolved strength of galvanized metal are known as "Steel Magnolias." I am the daughter, granddaughter, and niece of a large bouquet of those very blooms. I saw their loveliness in the graceful ways they carried themselves, in how they dressed for going to the market or for just sitting on the patio. But I was also witness to their most intense beauty during times that called on their steel. They balanced femininity and fortitude the way a butterfly balances itself with two wings. The right or wrong response from either wing can send you flying or falling.

In the context of this sisterhood, I was introduced to the potluck, and it became my template for community. My first memories were of aproned aunts scrambling for position in the kitchen; they worked for hours, and by the time morning gave way to afternoon, the refrigerator was full of the fruits of their labors. Creamed corn in a deep bowl looked up through plastic wrap on the shelf next to breaded okra. The corn had been shaved from the cob by my bony but pot-bellied oldest aunts over morning cigarettes and coffee. They mixed the corn with sweet milk and butter in the frying pan and cooked it until the sugars were released. The okra was washed, cut up, and dipped in egg, followed by a dusting of cornmeal. It would be fried in the same skillet as the corn was, just before we sat down to eat. My most flesh-endowed aunt snapped the sugar peas after opening her first Coke bottle of the morning. My morning Diet Coke drinking is clearly genetic in origin.

Arguing over whether to bake the buttermilk corn bread in an iron skillet or in muffin tins, my mom (the youngest) and her closest sister, Gene, huddled in muffled cackles, making comments under their breath about their older sister, Virginia, who told off-color jokes. By afternoon, muffins *and* skillet corn bread were piled up beside fried chicken on a platter covered in foil, and Aunt Virginia's "blue" joke had been retold a half-dozen times in quiet corners around the house. Mom's pale, yellow-tinted potato salad, bound with mustard instead of Nanny's Miracle Whip, completed the list of things to be prepared. After adding their own individual touches to the meal to come, the sisters sat down for a glass of sweet tea.

I can remember the smells settling over the house in the early afternoon, signaling that dinner was not far off. The uncles put the kitchen and card tables toe to head, and a patchwork of Pyrex dishes and Fiesta bowls, covered casseroles and dutch ovens, crockery and carnival glass was placed within reach of every diner. I loved the deviled-egg plate, with its egg holders arranged in concentric circles, and the relish trays that served up sweet pickles and olives. Every food was at home in its dish, and I was most at home in my skin at those tables.

At family gatherings during my childhood, when relatives arrived at the designated aunt's house, the initial conversation was a bit labored with the formality that accompanies distance and time. But as minutes became hours, the formality passed as one of my uncles pulled a dime out of my ear or dropped it from my nose. We all responded with proper amazement at the mystifying world of magic.

Next came the comments on how all the nieces and nephews had grown, inquiries about boyfriends or girlfriends, and reports on the various illnesses and "conditions" of the uncles and aunts. With the initial state-of-the-family reports out of the way, we settled into a comforting rhythm of conversation, shared lives, and easy presence. Someone always asked about my navy dad, what faraway port he was stationed in, or where his last letter was posted. Uncle George relayed the latest news about bicycle repair, Uncle Wigi shared a gruesome story from his surgical practice, pausing occasionally to puff on his pipe, and Uncle Jess discussed his latest business ventures. It wasn't the stuff of big-screen movies, just the stuff that lubricates time, making life slide from one day to the next.

Whatever home we were in, the sights, sounds, and smells were similar. In my mind, I can see the same scene repeating itself throughout the years. Aunts busied themselves in the kitchen, chopping onions, stewing greens, frying fish or chicken or corn bread. The life of the family swelled in its fullness to push against the walls and windows of the house. By the time the food was prepared and we sat down at the mix of tables, our family was comfortable again, familiar and safe. We filled our bellies with the endless parade of food and our hearts with what would become the best memories of my childhood.

We children were never deemed old enough to help with either the meal preparation or the cleanup. And although not being allowed to help did little to train us for when it would be our turn in the kitchen, it extended our childhoods generously. So, happy to be children and play after we ate, we moved to the carport to mount bicycles or go-carts, motorcycles or lawn tractors. Meanwhile, the aunts washed the dishes, and the uncles nursed their strange-smelling adult drinks on the back patio and talked about charcoal grills and gas mowers.

After the last crumbs were wiped from the fully extended table, the aunts settled in for an evening of canasta. An hour into the game, one or two aunts scooted back from the game table and fixed a glass of buttermilk with broken-up corn bread floating in it. Someone else shopped through the refrigerator and grabbed a piece of bread to fold over cold chicken. And soon the scent of leftovers floated throughout the house, beckoning everyone to return to the kitchen for plates of potato salad, okra, beans, and creamed corn. Uncles shimmied past aunts on their way to the refrigerator for more Husband's Delight, a favorite chocolate-pudding-cream-cheese-walnut-crusted dessert. By bedtime the sink was full of dishes again, but they could wait till morning.

Our family gatherings were warm times of reconnecting over dinner and games, preparation and cleanup, patio talks and go-cart rides. Important thoughts were shared and counsel was offered to those making decisions and life choices. Personal victories were celebrated and mistakes were teased. My older sister was relentlessly nagged about her dark eye makeup and long bangs—no one bothered to comment on her short skirts. But she held her head up, ironed her long and beautiful red hair, and added more mascara to the lashes peeking out from under her bangs. I thought she looked like the cover of a magazine. To this day, my sister is more resilient than I am, and maybe it's because she has been a steel magnolia for nine years longer than I have. Year after year our family potlucks were the place for skin to be toughened and hearts to be softened.

When Jim and I were first married, we joined my family for a reunion in Arkansas. We convened at our family cabin, a gathering place since my childhood. This would be our last time to go there before the cabin was sold. Aunts, uncles, cousins, grandchildren, sons-in-law, and daughters-in-law all made the journey "home" and collected by the sleepy lake spotted with cypress stumps. The cabin slept only a dozen, so the rest of us lodged in the clubhouse in dormitory-style rooms with single beds lining the walls. Jim and I suffered the heat and relentless ridicule and slept together in one single bed, our newlywed status still fresh.

Throughout our entire trip to the cabin—which entailed two plane rides and a long rental-car drive to the edge of nowhere—I described the food to Jim. In detail I told of the aunts and the full tables, the bulging refrigerators stuffed with Southern goodness, and the midnight leftover plates. "If nothing else," I promised, "the food will be outstanding."

When we got there, we pulled onto the lawn and parked. I was excited to see Mom and Dad, my sister and her husband, my cousin and her husband, and the smattering of aunts and uncles loitering about. As we walked into the cabin, we discovered that the topic of discussion in my sister's and cousin's cars had been much like ours, the women telling the husbands how amazing the food would be and how they wouldn't be disappointed.

But in the fading sunlight of that summer afternoon, the aunts unboxed deli potato salad and store-bought beans. Pale grocery-store-roasted chickens and bakery cakes lined the table, and paper plates and plastic forks were hastily piled high. Pill bottles and medicines sat on refrigerator shelves that had once held crockery full of homemade foods, and a strange collection of soft-spoken women seemed to have stolen our confident and boisterous aunts, inhabiting their frail bodies like alien predators. The collection of indefatigable sisters was tired, and the kitchen was closed.

That night, with no warning whatsoever, it became "our turn." Playtime was over for the cousins, and the torch was unceremoniously passed into our hands, recipes for cinnamon toast and tuna casserole the extent of our resources. There was no canasta that night, no midnight leftovers. Back in the dorm room, I quietly spooned under my new husband's arms in our cramped single bed, and that night I grew up against my will.

How would we pick up where our aunts left off? What were the tools for generational transition? It wasn't only that the food had always been good. And it wasn't just that the sisters had managed the tasks of feeding everyone and cleaning up. My youth had been filled with women in the kitchen modeling a way of life and relationship that I had only just started to know. I wasn't ready to lead; I had only begun to follow. Where were the recipes? Where were the safe places for figuring out how to be a grown-up? How would I navigate in my own empty kitchen?

Thanksgiving came two weeks after my mom died last year. Our typical traditions—where we gathered and what we ate—didn't feel right. The changes were coming faster than I could adapt to them, and what I had come to be comfortable with—my family template for the way things are supposed to be—was not lining up with my new reality.

Several days after the memorial service for Mom in Orlando, Jim and I went back to Nashville. I could only bear to leave my dad alone because we had agreed to meet the following week at my cousin's house in Atlanta for Thanksgiving.

When Jim and I got home, I could barely think about how to unpack my clothes, much less what to cook and take to Atlanta. My cousin called and said, "Just come. I'll take care of all the food."

I remembered all the times my mom had loaded my sister and me into a car at night to drive to one of my aunt's homes a few hours away because someone needed us. Someone was hurt, sick, or alone, and we would go to *be* with them. Kitchens filled up with sisters, living-room floors were littered with sleeping cousins, and family gave out of whatever we had. It was always a feast of food and love.

We drove to Atlanta in silence, my quiet weeping steaming up the windows. I knew the holiday would be melancholy, even if it was softened by being with those who loved Mom and me. My sister and her husband would be making their way to Texas, sharing old and new traditions in their daughter's home. Each of us would be in different kitchens, at different tables, and we would have to find a new way to be together.

When I got out of the car in Atlanta, my cousin Cindy came out of her garage to meet me. She held me, we cried, and she smelled of ham and potatoes and spicy chili. I walked into her kitchen and saw the counters filled with food and peeked into a refrigerator where a fat turkey was thawing. And I felt home beneath my unsure feet.

The next day when we gathered for our Thanksgiving meal, my widowed aunt and newly widowed dad balancing opposite sides of the table. Cindy and her husband, Greg, sat at the heads of the table, a perfect illustration of generational transition. The children's table had merged with the adults' table, and though our places had been rearranged, there was indeed a place for all of us.

We ate a plentiful meal—some new dishes, some traditional family ones. We told stories and remembered, and we mended a little bit. Corn-bread dressing was on our table, and when I talked with my sister, I found out that the same corn-bread dressing was on her table. The same dressing that had been on our tables every Thanksgiving all forty-six years of my life.

There isn't much to figure out in generational transition after all. When it's time, it just happens. After dinner Jim and my cousin's husband went to clean up the turkey smoker on the back patio, Diet Cokes in their hands. I leaned my head out the door and heard them talking about gas grills and riding lawn mowers. Dad and my aunt dozed in chairs in front of FOX News, and Cindy and I washed dishes, trying to remember how to play canasta. Over breakfast we would talk about new beginnings, and we would swap recipes, as we stepped up to take our turns.

# The Williams Sisters' Husband's Delight

### First Layer

    1 1/4 cups all-purpose flour
    1 stick butter, room temperature
    1 cup crushed walnuts

Preheat oven to 350 degrees. Mix ingredients together in a bowl, then press into 9 x 13 inch pie pan to form a crust. Bake 20 minutes. Set aside to cool.

### Second Layer

    1 cup powdered sugar
    1 (8-ounce) package cream cheese, softened
    1 cup whipped topping

Combine ingredients. Layer onto crust.

### Third Layer

    1 large box instant chocolate pudding
    3 cups milk

Mix together and add onto cream-cheese layer.

### Fourth Layer

    1 (8-ounce) container whipped topping

Spread onto pudding layer. Refrigerate before serving.

# CINDY'S THANKSGIVING PRETZEL SALAD

### First Layer

*3 tablespoons granulated sugar*

*3/4 cup butter*

*2 cups crumbled pretzels*

Preheat oven to 350 degrees. Mix ingredients and spread onto cookie sheet. Bake 15 minutes, stirring occasionally. Press into bottom of 9 x 13 inch baking dish to form crust.

### Second Layer

*1 (8-ounce) package cream cheese*

*1/2 cup powdered sugar*

*2 cups miniature marshmallows*

*12 ounces whipped topping*

Blend cream cheese and sugar, then fold in marshmallows and whipped topping. Spread over crust.

### Third Layer

*2 1/2 cups boiling water*

*1 box (6 ounces) strawberry gelatin*

*1 box (10 ounces) frozen strawberries*

*Fresh strawberries, for topping*

In a mixing bowl pour boiling water over strawberry gelatin and stir until dissolved. Stir in frozen strawberries. Let mixture set in refrigerator 2 hours, then add to baking dish. Refrigerate until firm. Cut fresh strawberries in half and lay them facedown on top of mixture as a garnish.

*Substitution Note:* You can substitute frozen raspberries or blueberries for the frozen strawberries. You can also substitute fresh banana slices for the strawberry topping.

## MOM'S CORN-BREAD DRESSING

*1 medium onion, diced*
*2 cups diced celery*
*1 pound sausage*
*2 pans corn-bread muffins (follow directions on bag of
   cornmeal)*
*4 cups chicken broth*
*salt and pepper, to taste*
*1 tablespoon poultry seasoning, or to taste*

Preheat oven to 350 degrees. Put onion and celery in saucepan
and cover with water. Boil until tender; do not drain. Brown
sausage in skillet; do not drain. Crumble corn bread in large
bowl. Mix in onion, celery, and liquid; sausage and any grease;
chicken broth; and seasonings. Add more chicken broth if the
mixture seems too dry. Pour into 9 x 13 inch baking dish. Bake
50 minutes, or longer if dressing seems too moist.

*Substitution Note:* In my nonmeat days, I left out the sausage and
just added more poultry seasoning. I also substituted vegetable
broth for chicken broth.

# FIRST CHURCH POTLUCK

*The Beauty of Being Found*

Family potlucks are my first memory of shared meals, but church potlucks are a close second. If aunts back home were the foundation for my understanding of community, monthly Wednesday night dinners at Huntwood Baptist Church in Long Beach, California, were the first-floor addition.

My dad was in the navy, and for many years he was stationed on a ship based out of the Long Beach Naval Base. This meant that my mom, my sister (Melani) and I were home without him for months at a time. Dad's family lived back east, and Mom's people were in the Deep South. Geographically displaced from the families who loved us, we felt a little lost. So we became regulars at Huntwood, attaching ourselves to the small congregation that faithfully gathered there.

I always dressed well for Sunday church. Before I could read and barely after I could count, I wore matching gloves, hat, and turned-down lace socks, and I carried a fashionable handbag. Most of these accessories were to detract attention from my scabby knees and elbows, signs of my fierce tomboy play. My Sunday-school teacher could hardly wait to explore my purse with me, itemizing the tissues, hard candy, small dolls, rubber frogs, and empty perfume bottles I had stuffed inside it.

This church was a place of spiritual and communal connection, a place where people knew our names and stories, a beginning legacy for our little family. Mom was a thirty-something woman with a preteen daughter (Melani) and a preschooler (me). She was not an anomaly for the era, since many women who married servicemen functioned for the most part as single parents. When the ships were home during the holidays, men in uniform spotted the pews of our little church, making it more obvious that there were others like us.

But when the ships were at sea and Dad was gone, the monthly potlucks at Huntwood became a featured part of our social world. Women crowded into the kitchen, while people of all ages crowded around tables, serving themselves from casserole dishes and Jell-O molds. The men asked Mom if the car was running all right and if she needed help mowing the grass. The ladies gathered me up on their laps and squeezed the cheeks of my perfectly round face. Everyone commented on how poised my sister was and what a young lady she was becoming. We looked forward to the Wednesday night potluck every day that week.

The Monday night before the potluck, Mom, Melani, and I sat at our Formica-topped dining-room table and searched through Mom's recipes, looking for that "just right" dish to take. For as long as I can remember, Mom had an oak recipe box that held 3 x 5 inch index cards. She scanned for recipes in her magazines, copied them meticulously onto the lined 3 x 5 cards, and stored them for later use. In the upper right-hand corner of each card, she carefully marked where her recipes came from, giving credit where it was due. The cards became a record of relationships, forever tied to flavors and foods—friendships formed over Wednesday night tables.

In the early 1960s, church potlucks were rich depositories of creamed and canned items, molded Jell-O salads, and marshmallowed Waldorf salads. Mom prided herself in preparing richly colored foods, the soft red of tomato aspic or the deep green of string beans with canned onion rings on top.

I couldn't read, but I could carefully separate the maybes from the noes as they were handed to me. Usually we started this process after evening dinner, the table freshly wiped down and the dishes drying in the rack on the counter. We discussed what had been our favorite recipes at last month's potluck and what ingredients we might have on hand for this month's recipe. As we sat under the frosted-glass-and-imitation-brass ceiling fixture, we mentally tasted spinach salad with mayonnaise and mandarin oranges, chicken and scampi, and rice consommé. We took great care to find a dish that would bring pleasure to the other diners. I will also admit that we were in pursuit of the occasional "Well done!" from our fellow potluckers.

While we searched and separated the index cards, the conversation inevitably wandered to Melani's homework, my favorite stuffed animals, news from Dad, and some new way Mom had found to clean something or to polish silver. These evenings were a ritual, a routine we nestled into each week that provided a familiar rhythm for our life.

Our Monday evening research turned into Tuesday preparation and Wednesday assemblage. Then Melani or Mom would smooth my fine blond hair into a high ponytail, and the three of us would put on shifts, or skirts with Peter Pan–collared shirts, and get into the pink station wagon to drive down to Huntwood. Along the way I stared out the window at other neighborhood kids, wondering if they had potluck families to belong to.

The church was always brightly lit, the parking lot filled with station wagons, people spilling out of all five doors. The linoleum-tiled fellowship hall echoed with busyness. Bare cafeteria tables were covered with mostly unmatching tablecloths brought from a variety of home linen closets; dishes were assigned to salad, entrée, or dessert tables. Someone was busy making the lemonade (California's version of sweet tea), and others were unfolding chairs for the increasing crowd.

I suppose there were only about one hundred of us at the most each month, but it seemed like an enormous crowd, the largest "family" gathering I had ever been to. Even so, chairs were always available, more than were needed. Welcomes need to be easy, and new people shouldn't ever have to get their own chairs.

I remember getting lost once at a potluck, a maze of legs and skirts at my eye-height in the fellowship hall. I started to panic until I saw the "Ann-blue" my mom so often wore and had indeed worn that night, and I attached myself to the dangling hem and the legs extending below it. When you are lost, you have to look for something familiar and risk attaching yourself to it. The woman, who was in fact not my mom, did not squeal but kindly *un*attached me and delivered me to my mom and sister, who were standing by the Lottie Moon missionary display near the lemonade pitchers.

Our band of three attached ourselves to the safe place that the Huntwood Baptist Church potlucks provided. Wednesday nights each month offered the approximation of family, the familiar welcome we longed for. If you felt a little lost, someone at the potluck would help you get found. And no one squealed if I grabbed hold of a hem.

We got home late on those Wednesday nights. There was always someone to talk with as we lingered in the parking lot, always someone to help carry our dishes to the station wagon. When we pulled up to our house, the sound of the garage door opening woke me just enough so that I could walk by myself into the house and to my bedroom. Those nights, I didn't need much help brushing my teeth or getting into my pajamas; I didn't need a bedtime story to calm my mind and prepare me for rest. In fact, there wasn't a lot of conversation in the house, because we were all talked out, all content, and all a little less lost and a little more found. Our chosen family had welcomed us again. As I drifted to sleep, I remembered that we would need to find a new recipe for next month.

## Mom's Chicken and Scampi

4 boneless, skinless chicken breasts
1 tablespoon salt
1/2 teaspoon pepper
1/4 cup butter
3 small onions, chopped
1 clove garlic, minced
3 tablespoons chopped fresh parsley
1/2 cup port wine
8 ounces tomato sauce
1 teaspoon dried basil
1 pound shrimp, peeled and deveined
yellow saffron rice, to serve

Season chicken well with salt and pepper. Melt butter in large skillet, then sauté chicken until golden on all sides. Add onions, garlic, parsley, wine, tomato sauce, and basil. Simmer covered about 30 minutes or until chicken is tender.

Push chicken breasts to one side of skillet and turn up heat so tomato mixture boils. Add shrimp. Reduce heat and cook uncovered 3–4 minutes or until shrimp is pink and tender. Serve with yellow saffron rice.

# THE VILLAGE CHAPEL

# POTLUCK

*An Old Tradition in a New Form*

After experiencing so many potlucks during my youth, now I am a grown woman hosting my own. I am offering welcomes, and finding welcomes, with a group of chosen family in Nashville, Tennessee. My husband is pastor of the Village Chapel, a new church with an interesting assortment of people. Some of us are tattooed or not, pierced or not, young or not; some are cynical, vulnerable, spiritually mature, or still uncertain. We are a collection of image bearers, each walking in our own story of grace by faith, and we try to balance our unity and diversity with charity.

The identifying phrase we use for the Village Chapel is "Rethinking church: new forms for ancient truths." We meet in a four-story, one-hundred-year-old nunnery, vacated by the sisters many years ago. It is three blocks from our home, in the center of a creative area of Nashville called Hillsboro

Village. In walking distance are Vanderbilt University, the Pancake Pantry, an old independent movie theater named the Belcourt, and a row of eclectic street shops and restaurants. The convent is all office space now, and we lease rooms on two floors. The chapel, which is used for various receptions and events, is completely ours on Sundays. The walls are soaked in ancient traditions, giving us a sense of connection to those who have gone before us.

Early in the formation of the Village Chapel, we decided to have a potluck. It seemed a rite of passage. Besides my own personal love of potlucks, it was an old tradition for gathering people together that needed reclaiming. The warmth and nostalgia of the practice offered a perfect place of connection for our young group. A week ahead of time, Jim invited everyone to bring a salad, an entrée, a side dish, or a dessert. The church would provide the utensils and drinks. (I secured a cooler of Diet Cokes.) Jim reminded everyone that Cheetos are not considered a side dish and encouraged people to make something for their party and four more people. Because of the eclectic personality of our group, I anticipated a wide expression of food to be present on our tables.

The night came for our potluck. April, a young woman who has made her heart available to the family at the Chapel, was in charge of setup. April has a deep love for the abundance of life and delightfully served us that afternoon as she directed the swarm of volunteers in dressing the historic chapel. Meanwhile, other volunteers filled coolers with ice and drinks or unfolded tables around the room and draped them in the disposable elegance of silver-colored plastic table-cloths. Suzanne, new to the church, brought flowers from her garden to arrange on every table.

We put candles on anything standing still. I had constructed rolling tables out of galvanized pipe and hot-water-heater trays. After spray-painting them with aluminum-colored paint, I arranged a half-dozen white-column candles in each tray. We placed the tables randomly throughout the room, along with four vintage wedding candelabra that I had scavenged from a thrift store. Those were spray-painted as well, and five tall white tapers sat across the tops of each, leaning at varying angles like teeth in a seven-year-old's mouth. We lit the wicks of all the candles in the room, signaling the beginning of something important and giving the room a glow that shined through the fifteen-foot-high windows and dripped onto the street below.

The hall filled with expectation as empty tables waited to be filled. Just after 6:00 p.m. the potluckers came, all anticipating, all responding in their own ways to the invitation to "come to the table." The hardwood floors creaked as they walked down the hall. Bedraggled or tidy, hesitant or sure, they brought their kitchen-crafted offerings.

The dishes were as varied as the potluckers, and as per Jim's instructions, there wasn't a bag of chips in sight. I skipped the entrée table and went straight for Ladawna's No-Bake Cookies, the decadent treat that beckoned my normally latent sweet tooth. Jan and Ric brought a traditional sweet-potato casserole, Suzanne and Mark set out pesto pinwheels, and I mixed up a vietnamese salad. Danny, Matthew, David, and James amazed us with their "single guy" cooking skills. We couldn't decide whether to put Carla's Lasagna Apple Pie on the entrée table or on the dessert table with Becky's Gammy's Pineapple Fluff Cake and Noelle's Gooey Maca-roon Pie. Mike and Nancy, who are experienced in crowds at the table because they have seven dogs, brought food *and* friends. The hungry had responded, they brought what they had to give, and the tables were overflowing. Perhaps the old tradition would be reclaimed in the candlelight of this ancient chapel after all. Perhaps the lost would be found; family would be chosen.

At the round tables, people began to settle in for eating. The bringers became receivers, and plates were piled with plenty. The room buzzed with conversations about recipes, stories about serving dishes that had been handed down from aunts and grandmothers, and tips on ways to successfully use ramen noodles. Unlikely table partners learned each other's names, and children ran through the maze of tables and chairs. I looked for the lost ones and tried to help them be found.

Generations of potluckers had gone before us, and this night, through our first-time potluck sacrament, it felt as if we officially became a church. Each bringing something, each taking something, and in the process becoming a community. I thought about Mom and my aunts, all but one now seated at a new table. I think they would have been pleased, despite the distinct lack of canasta playing. And I thought about the Wednesday night potlucks at Huntwood and how similar the welcome felt tonight. A new generation of potluckers was ushering in the tradition of belonging that is found in sharing meals, in breaking bread.

As Jim and I locked the chapel to leave, I popped open a final can of Diet Coke. "It was a good potluck, wasn't it?" I said.

"Yes, it was," he said.

Our two sets of footsteps echoed through the hall of the old building.

As we were driving the short trip to our house, Jim said he could imagine that the sleeping angels who resided in the upper reaches of the chapel had stretched and yawned tonight, waking up after the long years since the Saint Bernard sisters had been there. Perhaps they watched our ragamuffin band of diners, becoming seized by the power of a Great Affection, and said, "They're back. The family is home again."

# LADAWNA'S NO-BAKE COOKIES

*2 cups granulated sugar*

*1/4 cup cocoa*

*1/2 cup milk*

*1 stick butter or margarine*

*2 1/2 cups quick-cooking oatmeal, uncooked*

*1/2 cup peanut butter*

*1 teaspoon vanilla*

Combine sugar, cocoa, milk, and butter in a saucepan. Heat at medium high, stirring constantly. Once mixture reaches a full boil, boil exactly 1 1/2 minutes, stirring constantly. Remove from heat and add remaining ingredients. Stir well until completely blended. Drop by teaspoonfuls onto wax paper and let cool at room temperature. Mixture will set within 15 minutes. (Makes about 4 dozen.)

*Note:* This recipe requires precision in measurements. Also, don't make it in humid weather.

## JAN'S SWEET-POTATO CASSEROLE

3 cups cooked, mashed sweet potatoes
1 cup granulated sugar
1/2 teaspoon salt
2 eggs
3 tablespoons butter
1/4 cup milk
1 teaspoon vanilla

Preheat oven to 350 degrees. Mix ingredients and pour into greased 1-quart casserole dish.

### Topping

1 cup brown sugar, pressed
1/3 cup all-purpose flour
3 tablespoons butter
1 cup chopped pecans

Mix topping ingredients thoroughly and sprinkle over sweet-potato mixture. Bake 30 minutes.

# SUZANNE'S PESTO PINWHEELS

*1 cup packed fresh basil*

*3/4 cup pine nuts or almonds*

*2 large cloves garlic, minced*

*1/2 teaspoon salt*

*1/4 teaspoon pepper*

*3 tablespoons olive oil, divided*

*1/2 cup (2 ounces) grated parmesan cheese*

*1/2 cup (2 ounces) grated romano cheese*

*1/3 cup diced pimiento (optional)*

*2 (1-pound) frozen bread dough loaves, thawed*

Preheat oven to 375 degrees. To make the filling, combine basil, pine nuts or almonds, garlic, salt, pepper, and 2 tablespoons olive oil in blender or food processor. Blend or process until mixture is finely minced. Pour mixture into a bowl. Stir in parmesan cheese, romano cheese, and pimiento (if desired). Set aside.

Lightly grease a 9 x 13 inch glass baking dish. Roll each of the bread loaves into an 8 x 8 inch square. Brush squares lightly with the remaining olive oil. Spread half of filling on each square and roll up the square. Press dough together to seal the seam. Slice each roll into 8 pieces (16 total). Place cut sides up in the prepared baking dish. Cover dish and let dough rise until nearly double (approximately 45 minutes). Bake about 30 minutes or until golden brown. Cool slightly; remove from pan. Serve warm. (Makes 16 pinwheels.)

# BECKY'S GAMMY'S PINEAPPLE FLUFF CAKE

### Cake

> 1 box butter-flavored cake mix
> $1/4$ cup vegetable oil
> 3 eggs
> 1 can mandarin oranges, undrained

Preheat oven to 350 degrees. Beat cake mix, oil, and eggs as directed on cake-mix box. Stir in oranges and juice. Pour mixture into 2 greased and floured 9-inch cake pans. Bake following cake-mix directions or until toothpick inserted in center of cake comes out clean. Cool 10 minutes before removing from pans. Cool completely before adding icing.

### Icing

> 1 (12-ounce) container whipped topping
> 1 box vanilla instant-pudding mix
> 1 can crushed pineapple, drained

Combine all ingredients in order and chill two hours or until thoroughly chilled. Frost one layer, then place second layer on top. Finish by frosting sides and top. Chill for several hours before serving.

# NOELLE'S GOOEY MACAROON PIE

### Easy Yummy Crust

>    2 cups all-purpose flour
>    2 teaspoons granulated sugar
>    1/2 teaspoon salt
>    2/3 cup vegetable oil
>    4 tablespoons cold milk

Preheat oven to 350 degrees. Mix ingredients in a bowl, then knead mixture and press into 9-inch pie pan.

*Note:* This is a great recipe for any time you need an easy pie crust!

### Filling

>    2/3 cup granulated sugar
>    1 cup brown sugar, pressed
>    3 eggs
>    1 teaspoon vanilla
>    1/2 cup milk
>    2 tablespoons butter, softened
>    2/3 cup quick-cooking oatmeal, uncooked
>    1/2 cup chopped pecans
>    2/3 cup shredded coconut
>    whipped topping, to serve

Mix sugar, eggs, vanilla, milk, and butter with electric mixer. Stir in oatmeal, pecans, and coconut. Mix well. Pour mixture into pie shell and put foil around edges. Bake 40 minutes and remove foil. Bake approximately 5 more minutes or until mixture is set and light brown. Serve with whipped topping.

# SETTING A PLACE

*The Forgotten Are Welcome*

At a church potluck late last summer, I was walking around with a cup and a spoon, helping myself to a tiny serving at a time from each of the various dishes assembled on the table. This is part of my job as church mother, to sample from many dishes and be aware of their distinguishing characteristics. I sometimes forget their names but never their flavors.

I had just finished eating some of Sandy's Potato Salad and a pile of chips with Kari's Fresh Salsa when I looked up to see James walking into the chapel. In a vintage T-shirt topping narrow-legged jeans and brown wingtips, his tall frame passed easily across the room. He held a still-warm pot in a kitchen towel, and I made room in my cup for a small sampling of whatever it was. The dutch oven he carried bore witness to more than simply heated-up, canned ingredients. I anticipated something good.

"What have you brought for us, James?" I asked.

He lifted the lid and said, "Oh, I brought citrus beets. I like to work with the forgotten vegetables."

James is a single, thirty-something bass player, but it underestimates him to stop with that description. He is an intuitive musician, skillful in his craft and unusually attuned to the nature of a song. This is somewhat rare for someone who plays his particular instrument. Many times, a bass player focuses on the other rhythm instruments in an ensemble, but James is aware of the melody, the lyric, the decorative instruments, and even the vocalist. This soulful quality shows in his conversation as well. I remember the time James and I talked about the work of Spanish surrealist painter Joan Miró. He asked if I thought his color selection was symbolic or merely arbitrary? I made a mental note of James's multidimensional nature that was so unfettered by clichés.

Over the course of one fall a few years ago, James talked with Jim about faith issues that were unsettled in him. Jim complimented him on being an honest questioner, rather than a willful doubter, and helped put courage in his soul. Now James is leading the Saturday morning Village Chapel men's discussion of A. W. Tozer's book *Knowing God.* James is a man in pursuit of God, gathering with others on a similar expedition.

The tables were full at the potluck that night, and James's entry was a late one. Most people were advancing on their second helpings, and some were already making return visits to the dessert table. We were enjoying the long legs of summer light through the high-arched windows that Sunday. The lazy heat made people feel relaxed, and conversation buzzed like June bugs.

I am not a particular fan of beets, but James's dish smelled fresh and summery, and I determined that I was not going to pass up a "forgotten vegetable." I spooned a slice or two into my cup and tasted the tender-crisp, velvet-burgundy beets. The gentle citrus glaze made honest work of the beets, high-lighting their sweet root flavors. My own experience being favorable, I evangelized about the beets at each table I visited, and a respectable number of diners sought them out. The south end of the potluck table where the beets sat became busy with people motivated not by hunger as much as curiosity.

At the end of the evening, I watched a young man who was new to our potlucks. It was clear that he didn't know anyone, and by the way people were clumped, nobody had seemed to notice him. He stood mostly by himself, watching and smiling at conversations that were almost in reach, dis-cussions that almost included him.

The sky was dark by the time Jim and I locked up the building and walked to our car. The moon was low, and Mars was a bright presence that summer, glowing yellow compared to the white of the other faint stars. From our side of the nearly empty macadam parking lot, we saw James talk-ing to the young man I had seen standing alone during the potluck. I couldn't hear the entire conversation, but I heard

James say something like, "Why don't you come by my house, and we can go together?" And I thought of James's instinct toward forgotten things.

While we try to enfold the potluckers who come our way, there are always those who are forgotten, or less found than others. We'll keep setting a place for them, and someone will seek them out. It will probably be James.

## James's Orange-Glazed Beets with Currants

*3/4 cup currants or raisins*
*3/4 to 1 cup juice from two blood oranges (or another kind*
    *of orange)*
*3–4 medium-size fresh beets, scrubbed and peeled*
*2–3 tablespoons extra-virgin olive oil*
*1 large or 2 medium red onions*
*sea salt and freshly ground black pepper, to taste*

Place currants in small bowl. In a small saucepan, bring juice
from oranges to a boil, then immediately pour over currants.
Cover mixture.

Cut onions in half and then cut into six thick slices. Cut
beets in half and then cut each half into slices a bit thicker than
1/4 inch. (Beets can stain wood, so you might want to use a plastic
cutting board or sheet.)

In a heavy saucepan or large dutch oven (enamel-coated
cast-iron if you have one), warm olive oil (enough to amply cover
the bottom of the pan) over medium to medium-high heat. Stir
in beets and coat completely with oil. Reduce heat to medium
low, cover, and cook about 10 minutes, stirring every few minutes. (This is called sweating.) Add onion, stirring to coat evenly
with oil.

Cook until beets are nearly tender but not falling apart
(somewhere between 20 and 40 minutes). Add juice and currant

mixture. Salt and pepper to taste. Raise heat to medium high and cook uncovered, stirring until most of liquid has evaporated and a thick glaze has formed.

Great served hot or cold.

*Variations:* Like most recipes, this one can be adapted to your preferences or the ingredients on hand or in season.

- Apple juice can be substituted for the orange juice. Or you can substitute white or red wine and add a bit of fresh or dried tarragon during the final heating.
- A tablespoon or two of balsamic vinegar can be added to the juice.
- If the mixture is too tart, you can always add a little bit of sugar at the end. Or if you like a little extra kick, add a small amount of cayenne pepper at the end.

# Sandy's Potato Salad

*10 red potatoes, cubed*
*2 hard-boiled eggs, diced*
*2 bunches green onions, chopped*
*sliced radishes, for color*

Boil potatoes in salted water until tender. Combine all ingredients in large bowl.

### Dressing

*1¹/₂ cups real mayonnaise*
*²/₃ cup sour cream*
*1 tablespoon yellow mustard*
*paprika, several shakes*
*¹/₈ cup milk (adjust amount depending upon desired thickness)*
*salt and pepper, to taste*

Combine mayonnaise, sour cream, mustard, and paprika in container with a lid. Add milk until mixture is at desired consistency. Add salt and pepper. Shake dressing well. Pour over potato mixture and stir.

# KARI'S FRESH SALSA

*8–10 vine-ripened tomatoes, chopped and seeded*
*1 large white, yellow, or red onion, chopped*
*4–6 cloves garlic, finely chopped*
*1 jalapeño pepper, seeded and diced*
*1 can green chilies, drained and chopped*
*1/2 cup fresh cilantro, chopped*
*juice from 2 limes*
*1/3 cup olive oil*
*2 tablespoons red-wine vinegar*
*salt and pepper, to taste*

Combine tomatoes, onion, garlic, pepper, chilies, and cilantro in large bowl. Add lime juice, oil, and vinegar. Add salt and pepper to taste. Chill in refrigerator 2 hours before serving to let flavors mingle.

*For a spicier salsa:* Mix 1 1/2 teaspoons ground cumin with 1 can chipotle peppers in adobe sauce, and purée in food processor. Add to salsa.

# SNACK POTLUCK

*Life Is Messy, but It's Worth It*

The Village Chapel women recently came to my house for a snack potluck and a discussion on the topic of "significance." Nancy brought some girly cucumber-and-cream-cheese finger sandwiches on thin wheat bread. (She and I were quite entertained by them because, in fact, neither of us is a "girly" girl.) Carla brought the requisite chocolate brownies, without which we would simply have had to cancel the gathering. Joyce brought homemade bread, and the other women brought cookies, muffins, fruits, and nuts.

Joyce and her husband, David, have been part of the Village Chapel for three years now. We lovingly refer to them as "seasoned" attendees, as we refer to anyone who is over forty and finds his or her way to the Chapel.

Since the first Christmas I met Joyce, I have been a fortunate recipient of her cooking. Around the holidays each year, Joyce power-bakes multiple loaves of her specialty cake-like breads. These are not the everyday breads of sandwiches or soup partnering; they are "jewelry" accents, designed to be savored like bonbons. When wrapped in festive paper, they make perfect little holiday packages. I eat them respectfully.

When Joyce is in full seasonal production, different bowls and ingredients are spread across her black granite–topped kitchen counter. Pecans, cranberries, bananas, and poppy seeds wait to be folded into dough that must be muscled to mix. Lemon, vanilla, almond, and other extracts scent the breads—I picture all the ingredients sitting out like crayons in a sixty-four-count box, waiting to be selected and colored with. After baking, the loaves are released from greased pans onto racks where they will set. Once the loaves cool, sticky plastic wrap provides a protective skin before the bread is dressed in holiday wrapping paper.

While I am delighting in the precious snack gifts at my house, Joyce is still cleaning up her kitchen. The mess created by her labor of love takes much longer to clean up than it did to make. Bits of dough have been flung as far as the living room, and the family cat enjoys the dried cranberries that have strayed underneath the dining-room table. Joyce is meticulous in her craft, as she is in everything she applies her-self to. If I were in charge of handing out gold stars, Joyce would get one, or perhaps a few dozen.

Joyce and David have been married just shy of thirty years. He is an anesthesiologist, and she was a nurse until she had her babies. Then she turned her focus to raising the three girls and did it with the same careful attention she applied to nursing. Her list of talents and accomplishments is long, but Joyce's deepest waters run from her love of Bible history and archaeology. With gracious confidence, she passes along to the rest of us the wisdom she has gleaned in these areas. She also knits with tiny, barely visible knitting needles and decorates her home in my favorite minimalist style.

At the snack potluck, Joyce's bread and the many other offerings eased us into the evening. My friend Margaret and I, as hosts, gently coaxed the dialogue. We had asked the women to bring an item from home that symbolized what gives them a sense of personal significance. Each woman took a turn introducing what she brought. The items became symbolic curtains to safely hide behind, allowing us to reveal ourselves to one another a little at a time.

Two professional women brought work IDs and business cards, indicating that they get their significance from their jobs and their titles. One young woman brought her hands, because the things she makes with them give her significance. A new bride brought her husband's wedding ring—"His love has given me significance." One young single woman shared a photo of her friends, other women spoke about their relationships, and several referred to their appearance as sources of personal significance. I was struck by the wisdom of the thirty women who sat in my home. Each of them shared something out of honest reflection and vulnerability.

When it came to Joyce's turn, she reached into her purse

for a plastic baggy. As she pulled it out and retrieved the item inside, I could see the silver tangle, glazed in blue soap. It was a steel-wool scouring pad.

"I clean up messes," she started. She talked about cleaning until her knuckles are white and how the satisfaction of a room well cleaned lends her personal significance. She spoke of the messes she cleaned up as a nurse, and as a wife and mother, and she referred to the various tools of the trade: scrub brushes, gloves, sponges, and scouring pads.

Then Joyce pulled back the curtain some more, exposing the personal side of her symbol. She spoke about the messes we all make in our lives, and about some of the specific ones that have cost her tears. With a respectful balance of vulnerability and privacy, she spoke of the ache of disappointment and the exhaustion that comes with the simple fact that life is messy, though we do our best to clean it up. In her soft-spoken way, she smiled at the challenge, and I pictured her in her apron, fervently wiping up spills and scrubbing the baked-on messes in bread loaf pans.

Like Joyce, I prefer messes I can actually clean up, the kind of cleanup that results in things being restored to the way they were before. But life is full of uncontrollable messes that will not be cleaned this side of heaven, no matter how hard we scrub and scour.

Joyce's neatly packaged breads in holiday costume give no hint of the messes made in creating them. But being aware of the mess makes the bread more special to me. It is the same with lovely Joyce. Her neat and tended exterior gives little evidence of the life messes she has survived. I barely see the faint residue in her eyes, but knowing about a few of her messes makes her all the more important to me.

As the women collect themselves to leave at the end of the evening, I gather leftovers from the table. There are no brownies, but residuals of cookies, sandwiches, nuts, and bread get tucked into Ziploc baggies or Tupperware containers for another day. The women have also left bits of themselves, pieces that showed their hearts. I tuck those away too.

I finish cleaning up the mess left behind after everyone leaves, and soon the room looks the way it did before the evening began. I polish the top of my dining-room table and put away the last of the chairs. Most of the evidence of the ladies' presence is gone, except for the minimal trash I bag up and set at the back door. I determine that the mess is a small price for the goodness of the evening. Perhaps that's what I will take from our snack potluck tonight. That and a few slices of Joyce's bread.

# JOYCE'S POPPY-SEED BREAD

*3 cups all-purpose flour*
*2 cups granulated sugar*
*3 eggs*
*1 1/2 teaspoons baking powder*
*1 1/2 teaspoons salt*
*1 1/2 tablespoons poppy seeds*
*1 1/2 cups milk*
*1/4 cup vegetable oil*
*1 1/2 teaspoons vanilla extract*
*1 1/2 teaspoons almond flavoring*
*1 1/2 teaspoons butter flavoring*

Preheat oven to 350 degrees. Combine ingredients and beat
2 minutes. Spoon batter into 2 greased and floured loaf pans and
bake 1 hour or until toothpick comes out clean. Let loaves cool
in pans 10 minutes, then turn loaves onto wire racks to cool
completely before adding glaze.

### Orange Glaze

*1 cup powdered sugar, sifted*
*2 tablespoons orange juice*
*1/4 teaspoon vanilla extract*
*1/4 teaspoon almond flavoring*
*1/4 teaspoon butter flavoring*

Mix ingredients together and drizzle over cooled bread.

# NEW YEAR'S EVE POTLUCK

## *Incarnational Soup*

Carmen welcomed us at the front door as the steam from our mouths mingled with our "hellos." Everyone brought something that night. There was homemade corn bread still warm in the foil; a green salad with dried fruit, nuts, and cheese; and a plate piled with double-chocolate brownies. Weary from holiday comings and goings, we also brought our tired souls, dragging them behind us over the threshold of Carmen's front door.

Carmen made chicken soup for all of us that New Year's Eve. She is the incarnation of Christ's most empathic heart. Her eyes see the pain and suffering people carry, and after you have spent time with her, you leave lighter, having had your burden shared. Sometimes Carm is quiet and just nods her head as you spill out your weariness before her. Other times, when you can't find the words for your ache, she ably finds her voice and lends solidarity to your silent hurt. Like the time she screamed "No, no, no…" into the phone when

I called to tell her that my mom had cancer and was dying. With that single-word lament she brokered my pain, negotiating on my behalf the anger and claustrophobic fear that left me mute.

I met Carmen when she started dating our dear friend Jeff. After pizza that first night, we pulled Jeff aside and said, "This is the one; don't let her go." About a year later I sat in the high-ceilinged church while Jim ushered people to the side of the bride or groom. Ironically, there I was on the bride's side even though I'd known Carm for far less time than Jeff. But old souls connect with ease, and Carm and I are old souls.

We would come to share a lot of life over the next few years. Jim and I would meet to play dominoes at their place, or gather for a small Bible study the four of us started, or go to a movie and dinner.

I remember the time Carmen and Jeff invited us over to eat homemade pasta. They had spent the afternoon tediously making the pasta, and when we got there, we went into the kitchen to admire it. It had been laid out on a cloth on the table like thin sheets of butter-colored porcelain. As I waved my arms in enthusiastic anticipation, I tangled my hand in the glass hummingbird hanging from the pull string of the ceiling fan. When I jerked my hand back to untangle my fingers, I sent the hummingbird flying up into the fan blades, where it met with an untimely decapitation. The poor bird shattered into salt-sized pieces that fell like rain all over the homemade pasta. Without missing a breath, the ever-adaptable Jeff said,

"Jim, let's go over to Kroger and pick up a box of pasta."
Meanwhile, Carm and I stayed behind and disposed of the
evidence of my encounter with the now headless hummingbird. She said she thought the flavor of boxed pasta was actually far superior to homemade—and didn't I agree?

The four of us spent Carm and Jeff's first married
Thanksgiving together at their condo, and I gifted them with
horribly ugly ceramic-turkey salt-and-pepper shakers. The
table was already set with fine china and crystal wedding
pieces. Gravy boats and cut-crystal bowls, bone-china plates
and water goblets that rang when you thumped them on the
edge, silver serving pieces and lead-crystal candle holders
mapped out the loveliness of the holiday. Carm placed the
ceramic turkeys in the middle of that loveliness. I love that
about her. In her economy, fine china and crummy ceramics
are perfectly appropriate tablemates.

Now, after the birth of their two children, after a decade
and a half of birthdays, holidays, tragedies, celebrations, losses,
and gains, there we were, assembled with a few more friends
at a table that had become almost as familiar as my own. The
corn bread, salad, soup, and brownies before us had been
assembled in many kitchens by many hands and were spread
out across the table as a reflection of the people who sat ready
to receive them. We had all negotiated the Christmas holidays with family, friends, and professional acquaintances.
Some of us were in a fine-china season of life, some of us were
in a simple ceramics season, and some of us were chipped

pottery, needing to be glued back together. As always, there was a place for each of us at Carm and Jeff's table.

With years of familiarity, we found an easy rhythm of conversation. It was a generous crowd, and everyone felt comfortable speaking of recent accomplishments or challenges, equally engaged by the eyes around the table. We discussed the kinds of issues that always surface at the change of the year: finances, career changes, uncertainties. Carmen kept a watchful eye on our bowls, careful to provide refills when they were empty or nearly empty, the way the ocean sand fills in when you lift your foot out of it. Red Christmas candles burned smokelessly throughout the evening, soundlessly reducing themselves to nearly flat discs of wax as the hours escaped.

Carm's soup nurtured our souls and warmed our bellies. Perhaps it was a bit like the eucharistic host that evening, becoming the body of Christ to our little gathering and reminding us that we were loved and chosen. We came to the table empty, and we would leave filled again.

In a fragile pause between when the soup bowls sat empty and the dessert dishes were yet to be covered with brownies, one of the couples began to share about their prodigal son. The shards of their broken hearts ripped through their quiet demeanors. A few sparse details gave us enough to glimpse the depth of their sadness. We inhabited the pause, the moment of unspoken empathy, and then each of us stood and walked over to our friends to put our arms around them.

Gathering around them for the love of their son, we prayed for mercy.

The awkward moment following such vulnerability was brief, and then the dessert tray filled with brownies was passed around. The brownies almost gone, conversation turned back to movies or books or new CDs. We didn't dwell on the prodigal son, but later, each of us would whisper his name in our own private prayers.

As we pushed away from the table for the last time that year, chocolate-covered mouths were wiped on the white linen napkins that had dried our tears that night.

After everyone had gathered coats and serving dishes on the way out the door, I worked in the kitchen with Carm for a while. As we readied the bowls and plates for the dishwasher, Carm and I talked quietly, about nothing and everything.

"Your soup was really good tonight, Carm."

"Oh, it was the same as it always is, Kim."

*Exactly,* I thought.

We came with full dishes and nearly empty souls and left with empty dishes and near-full souls. As always, Carm was an agent of mercy that evening, gathering us in from the cold. Soup was just her cover.

## CARMEN'S PORTUGUESE CHICKEN SOUP

*5 pounds chicken thighs (with bones and skin)*

*4 quarts water*

*2 medium white or yellow onions, peeled and quartered*
 *(reserve 1/4)*

*3 carrots, halved*

*1 head garlic, chopped (reserve 3 cloves, chopped)*

*1 celery stalk, chopped (reserve 2 tablespoons)*

*1 bay leaf*

*1 teaspoon dried thyme (if fresh, use a few sprigs)*

*fresh parsley, a few sprigs*

*8 whole, black peppercorns*

*apple-cider vinegar, to taste*

*salt, to taste*

*1 cup egg noodles, uncooked (or rice, if desired)*

In a large stockpot, combine chicken with water, vegetables, and herbs. Bring to a boil, skimming off scum that rises to the surface. Reduce heat and simmer 30 minutes, skimming periodically. Strain mixture and reserve broth. Strip chicken meat from bones and return meat and reserved broth to stockpot. Bring mixture to a simmer and add chopped, reserved vegetables. Add salt to taste. Add apple-cider vinegar by teaspoonful to taste. Add egg noodles (or rice, if desired) and simmer until cooked. (Serves 4–6.)

*Variations:* Experiment with fresh mint, a little lemon zest, or rosemary. If desired, add more parsley and thyme. For creamier soup, add 1/2 cup half-and-half after adding the vinegar. If you are serving the soup without noodles or rice, try adding chunks of avocado or a poached egg to each serving. Or you can serve the soup over lightly toasted, thick-cut bread.

# A NEW WELCOME

*The Power of Second Chances*

The potluck became an instant tradition at the Village Chapel. An unspoken bond united us in unexpected ways at those tables of collective offerings. The MAC Cosmetics girls found themselves sharing a table with the auto-parts salesman and his wife and two children. And the piano teacher found conversation with the MTV audio engineer.

Jodi brought Lime-Loaf to our third potluck. It was a strange dining experience for the cappuccino-drinking, used bookstore–browsing, vintage clothing–wearing, pierced, tattooed, and dreadlocked congregation that gathered for a meal that night. It was also unusual for the khaki, golf-shirted crew in attendance.

If I tell you about Jodi, the dish she chose to bring will seem less odd. Every week Jim and I meet Jodi and her husband, Brad, for Taco Tuesday to discuss life and the significant and insignificant goings-on of our days. (The name comes from our first meeting place: a neighborhood Mexican restaurant. We moved Taco Tuesday to a café in a bookstore for a while, and most recently to an Italian restaurant, but we still affectionately call it Taco Tuesday.)

Jodi and Brad own a consignment store with a faithful local clientele, which I have recently joined. They sell everything from mink coats to shoes, and although the six-thousand-dollar minks never come home with me, a plethora of twenty-dollar items have found their way to my closet.

The Lime-Loaf experience started when Brad and Jodi found some books in the piles of clothing a client dropped off for resale. They do not sell books at the store, so it is a bit of a mystery why the books showed up at all. Most likely, piles got mixed together on a spring-cleaning day at the client's home. However it happened, a quirky potluck cookbook from an old Methodist church landed at Designer Renaissance and in my friends' hands.

That night at Taco Tuesday, we scanned the pages looking for potential recipes. I had to reach for the reading glasses dangling around my neck in order to read the typewriter-pecked-out pages, but we delighted in this new cache of potluck resources. Produced in 1965, the cookbook included such recipes as Tomato Pudding, Orange Candy Cake, and the aforementioned Lime-Loaf. Amid the dog-eared, thread-bare, and tomato-sauce-stained pages were the quaint, personal recipes of real people who had brought real dishes to be shared by this real Methodist community more than forty years ago. To be honest, Jodi and I questioned some of the obscure pairings in a few of the recipes. We had never used the words *tomato* and *pudding* in the same sentence, much less to describe the same food.

Jodi and Brad live in an urban neighborhood near downtown Nashville, around the corner from a popular comedy club and a collection of antique shops. The houses are still just barely affordable, and the charm of earlier decades marks the individual bungalows and cottages. Some signs of urban "renewal" have begun to bruise the aesthetic, like when a historic neighborhood church gave way to multiunit town houses clothed in vinyl siding. Many of the older residents are moving on to retirement centers, leaving their houses to sit empty until a new family sees the potential in reclaiming the real estate.

Jodi and Brad married a little later in life, and they share a love for things marked by wear but not beyond rescue. They met in a church choir a few years after Jodi had been through a difficult divorce. They fell in love and were married in less than a year. Their 1920s Southern bungalow keeps Brad busy patching and restoring, and the rooms are decorated with antiques and comfortable vintage fabrics. Their old pickup truck serves them and their friends and is parked between their vintage Alfa Romeo and their five-year-old Volvo. Their store has provided second chances for every type of clothing, from wedding dresses to sundresses, spandex and leather to cashmere and pearls. The second floor of their home is almost always occupied by a friend or acquaintance who is between homes and needs a safe nest in which to repair a broken wing or two. Their dogs, Casey and Baxter, patrol their fenced backyard. Casey, a Weimaraner, and Baxter, a PoGo (standard poodle/golden retriever), both had previous owners. Brad and Jodi are champions of the second chance.

Two of the key ingredients of Lime-Loaf are crumbled vanilla-wafer cookies and shredded coconut browned in butter. The other key ingredient for which Lime-Loaf was named is lime Jell-O. Trust me, Brad and Jodi's Lime-Loaf didn't make a pretty presentation that night at the potluck. But one spoonful sent you back to the dessert table to serve up a proper portion, and inspired testimonials from Lime-Loaf converts brought unbelievers to the loaf. I myself had written anything Jell-O off my list some time ago. But this night, a second chance revealed that I had overlooked some lovely qualities in properly prepared gelatin.

If "new forms for ancient truths" is to have any relevance for us at the Village Chapel, perhaps it will begin at our potluck tables. At these tables old and new mingle, the cream-of-something casserole sitting next to tofu burgers, and roasted vegetables and Thai salad sharing space with a nostalgic Lime-Loaf made from a 1965 Methodist cookbook recipe.

Jodi did not take home an empty dish that night, but that was okay with her. It wasn't about the quantity of Lime-Loaf eaten; it was about giving something that had been set aside another try. New and adventurous things at the potluck are nice, but I think there is an inherent goodness to something getting a second shot at the table. Maybe tired souls will drag themselves to the dinner and find refreshment in a new welcome from a familiar face.

Brad and Jodi's Lime-Loaf recipe was a kind of second-chance homily, illustrated in Jell-O, coconut, and cookies, served up in a meatloaf pan. I sat it on my plate next to a more glamorous macadamia-and-white-chocolate-chip cookie. They looked lovely together, and I ate them both. The cookie wasn't a stretch for me—I already knew I would like it—but the Lime-Loaf was a risk, as all second chances are.

# BRAD AND JODI'S LIME-LOAF

*1 cup shredded coconut*
*1 stick butter*
*1 cup crushed vanilla wafers*
*1 box lime Jell-O*
*1 cup hot water*
*2/3 cup granulated sugar*
*2 tablespoons lemon juice*
*8 ounces maraschino cherries, chopped*
*1 cup chopped pecans*
*1 cup heavy cream, whipped*

Brown coconut in butter and stir in crushed vanilla wafers.
Sprinkle half of mixture in bottom of oblong loaf pan and
reserve other half for topping.

Dissolve Jell-O in hot water and add sugar and lemon juice.
When Jell-O begins to thicken, add cherries and nuts. Fold in
cream and spread on top of coconut mixture. Sprinkle remaining
coconut mixture on top. Chill well before serving. This dessert is
good as long as it lasts!

*Note:* It takes a little while to brown the coconut, but the distinctive flavor is well worth the effort.

# An Honest Little Cake

*The Virtues of Imperfection*

Jim has a very good grip on who he is and what his gifts and limitations are. While he can untangle the knots of many philosophical conundrums, he does not attempt to enter my studio, pick up a brush or pencil, and express a latent artistic ability. He is master of the stick figure only—and not at all ashamed.

He is, however, quite good at a number of other things, not the least of which is being my husband. He understands where I keep myself, and he has learned to follow the breadcrumbs to my soul. He is also a caring pastor and a graceful and effective teacher. I like to refer to him as the "mama bird" because he is so good at going out and finding food, chewing it up, and then feeding it to us in a way that we can all digest. I'm aware that most men would prefer being referred to as a "roaring lion," a "cunning tiger," or even a "raging bear." But Jim finds the truth and beauty in my mixed-species, mixed-gender metaphor and wears it with gentle pride.

Jim is also patient and wise, has a good sense of humor, and can dance to the beat. And though he cannot cook, he can bake. For this wife, that falls under the "for richer" part of the marriage vows.

The ability that allows Jim to unpack challenging ideas and philosophies also equips him to follow a recipe with precision. When it comes to baking, mind you, this is an essential requirement. That is why I am a better cook than a baker—I like to improvise my way through a recipe. I enjoy substituting ingredients and experimenting with how things are seasoned or cooked. I often wade into foods I am uncertain about just for the sake of experiencing the newness.

But Jim can explain the difference between fudgelike brownies and fluffy cakelike brownies. "It's in the number of eggs you use," he says. Evidently, there is a certain chemical "thing" that happens when you add an extra egg, and the fluff factor is enhanced. It is a direct cause-and-effect situation in which Jim feels completely at home. He also understands the baking-powder-versus-baking-soda issue, is judiciously aware of the appropriate use of self-rising flour versus regular flour, and he would never add cold water to a recipe that called for hot water. I might add water at whatever temperature was handy at the time, and that is why my baked goods are far inferior to Jim's.

Jim officially took over the baking responsibilities in our marriage the morning after I served sawdust Hello Dollies to our guests. I was in a hurry and forgot to add the butter to the graham-cracker crust. Needless to say, things did not go well for me—or the recipe. Ironically, my dessert looked beautiful in the pan, but it would not traverse the evening on looks alone. It was only as I tried to cut and serve the squares that the failed crust beneath the lovely coconut-and-chocolate veneer was revealed. People struggled to affirm me by commenting on how good the other layers tasted, and how this sawdust situation could have happened to anyone. But that is where they were wrong. It would not have happened to Jim, because he follows the recipe. He has rarely served anything resembling sawdust to a guest, and if he has, it's because that's what the recipe told him to do.

While Jim maintains a vast repertoire of dessert creations, the one he is most known for in our circles is Jim's Ugly Chocolate Cake. It started out as a pleasant enough sheet cake, a moist chocolate dessert that doesn't get junked up by trendy ingredients or techniques. It's from a family recipe, and I remember it from holidays and company days when I was a child. Mom would make the chocolate cake and a spice cake, both in long cookielike pans that made serving them so very user friendly. The chocolate cake was my favorite, but I also loved the spicy oatmeal cake with the coconut and almonds in the frosting. So I always attempted an equitable distribution of each kind of cake on my plate. When I married, I made the cakes for Jim a few times, and his overwhelming favorite was the chocolate. So the spice-cake recipe is now used on those occasions calling for something nonchocolate. In other words—hardly ever.

When I relinquished my baking duties to Jim, he took the chocolate sheet-cake recipe and made it his own. He did not attempt to change or adjust any of the measurements or ingredients; he merely reinterpreted the form of the cake. Instead of baking it as a stretched-out sheet cake, Jim stacks it high by baking it in two round nine-inch pans. That is what logical recipe followers are comfortable with adjusting, the part that has little effect on the flavor of the baked item. Stacking a cake that was originally designed to be a sheet cake means that it rarely comes out perfect. It is usually lumpy looking, and the frosting lays like thin Lycra stretched over less-than-tight abdominals. But it remains an honest little cake and holds its own against prettier ones. People will, in fact, fight their way to the potluck table for Jim's Ugly Chocolate Cake. Searching my memory, I cannot remember anyone ever complaining, "If only the cake looked pretty, it would taste better!" Actually, an uneventful or disappointing evening at the experimental entrée table can be quickly forgotten with a bite of ugly but dependable chocolate cake. During one potluck, a carefully stylish and lip-glossed girl wore a chocolate-icing ring around her mouth from her encounter with the cake. The ring lingered long after the cake was gone, and when the girl smiled she looked vaguely like a sock monkey.

You can always count on Jim's cake to taste good each time he makes it. It is bona fide and dependably Jim's chocolate cake—and it's ugly. But it is a reminder that goodness is often hidden behind an imperfect exterior. Appearances of all kinds are welcome at the potluck. And we must never let a little "ugly" keep us from experiencing what is good.

# JIM'S UGLY CHOCOLATE CAKE

*2 cups granulated sugar*

*2 cups all-purpose flour*

*4 tablespoons cocoa*

*2 sticks butter*

*1 cup hot water*

*1/2 cup buttermilk*

*1 teaspoon baking soda*

*1 teaspoon vanilla extract*

*2 large eggs*

Preheat oven to 350 degrees. Sift together sugar, flour, and cocoa in medium-sized bowl. Set aside. In medium saucepan, bring butter and hot water to boil. Pour over sifted ingredients and mix.

In a separate bowl, mix together buttermilk, baking soda, vanilla extract, and eggs. Stir into cocoa mixture and pour into 2 greased and floured 9-inch cake pans. Bake about 20 minutes, until toothpick inserted comes out clean. Allow to cool 20 minutes before frosting.

### Icing

*1 stick butter*

*4 tablespoons cocoa*

*1/3 cup milk*

*1 pound powdered sugar*

Bring butter, cocoa, and milk to a boil, then remove from heat. Add powdered sugar, mixing well until sugar is dissolved. Frost first layer of cake. Stack second layer on top and finish frosting entire cake.

# DIVIDED PLATES

*Respectful Distinctions, but No Walls*

First the carrots, then the peas, then the ham, and finally the baked apples. I have a friend who eats all the food on her plate in sections only. There is no mingling or "polluting" of flavors, only separate and well-controlled tastings.

She would like the divided Styrofoam plates Jim bought for one of our potlucks. Jim is not very particular about such details and would be happy with divided or undivided plates. He is easily agreeable. I am, however, less agreeable, and I am not a fan of the divided plate. I quietly celebrated when the divided plates ran out and we were able to purchase the free-range, open plates. I enjoy an interlacing of flavors. I like the surprise of cranberry sauce interrupting my mashed potatoes and gravy on my plate at Thanksgiving. Or a pool of balsamic vinegar meandering from my salad to my green beans, flavoring them with unexpected poignancy. Some of my favorite recipes mingle unexpected flavors like curry and apples, coconut and chicken, currants and eggplant.

I can understand the logic behind the divided plates and can even see why they might be particularly appropriate for potluck dining. In a friendly tone, they clarify any confusion one might have at the serving table. "Here, my friend, is where you put your peas, and here your carrots, and your ham may sit comfortably in this large area," says the divided plate. This could be helpful for those who are overwhelmed by the choices and serving sizes at the potluck table, or for anyone who does not want to risk compromising the originally intended flavors.

I appreciate the desire to taste foods within the context of their own ingredients, and I am glad for those who prefer to eat off divided plates. I celebrate their freedom to do so. Perhaps it is because I am a seasoned potluck diner and find myself comfortable with the experience after so many years that I prefer the undivided plate. Having served myself from many tables, I know that there is no universal serving size and that it is perfectly acceptable to serve oneself five small entrées, bypassing the salads, or vice versa. For someone such as myself, divided plates confine rather than clarify.

In fairness, some foods need to be segregated out of respect for their distinctions. I am not a fan of hot dogs with bananas, or ice cream with sauerkraut; some things are dignified by giving them separation. On the whole, though, at our potlucks I hope we have respectful distinctions, but no walls.

What we rub up against in life helps define us, and artificial walls inhibit that possibility. While our unique differences must be respected, the benefit of iron sharpening iron happens in relationships, in a willing subjection to friction. Isolating ourselves behind the seeming safety of barriers leaves us unsharpened, dull, and flavorless. But risking relational proximity can actually result in something unexpected, something showing us that there are far fewer things separating us than uniting us.

# KIM'S CURRIED CHICKEN AND APPLE POT PIE

*2 refrigerated pie crusts*
*1 cup cubed red-skinned potatoes*
*1 tablespoon extra-virgin olive oil*
*1 pound boneless, skinless chicken breast, cubed*
*1 cup diced celery*
*1 cup sliced carrots*
*1 cup chicken broth*
*1/4 cup all-purpose flour*
*2 tablespoons curry powder*
*1/2 teaspoon salt*
*1 Golden Delicious apple, peeled and cubed*
*1/2 cup coconut milk*

Preheat oven to 425 degrees. Roll out one pie crust on wax paper and press into 9 x 13 inch baking pan. Precook crust 5–10 minutes, until almost golden. Roll out second crust on wax paper and set aside for top of pie.

Boil potatoes until just tender-crisp, then drain. In a separate pan, sauté chicken, celery, and carrots in olive oil. Cook until chicken is opaque, not pink. In a bowl, whisk together chicken broth, flour, curry powder, and salt. Pour into pan with chicken and vegetables. Add potatoes and bring to a boil. Stir in apple. Reduce heat and cook until sauce thickens, stirring constantly. Remove from heat and stir in coconut milk.

Pour mixture on top of pie crust in baking pan, then lay second rolled-out crust over top of pie. Crimp edges to seal tightly. Cut slits in top for steam to escape. Place pie on cookie sheet and bake 20–25 minutes, or until top is golden brown.

# Root Vegetables

## *Life from Dark Places*

Spring—the season of new life and the promise of hope. The reemergence from darkness to light. Warm days, blue skies, low humidity, and the sudden appearance of stout crocuses that dress the naked landscape in purple blooms.

Spring also ushers in the need I have to dig in my garden. I want to plant something, start something, pull up the dead and failed attempts and replace them with possibility. I want to rake redemption into the dark soil of winter. Every spring I purchase new garden gloves and put them in the basket on the shelf above my dryer. Then I forget about them and pull weeds with bare hands until a rash appears on my fingers and Jim asks where my gloves are.

The farmer's market opens in May, but in that last month of spring, you will find only salad greens, pale and flavorless strawberries, cabbage, cauliflower, and the star of the season: carrots. The bright orange vegetables are almost surreal in the density of their color. And carrots are not just a pretty face.

In a typical American diet, carrots are the principle source of vitamin A, which comes from beta carotene, a member of the group of plant pigments known as carotenoids, so named because they were first discovered in carrots. Good job, carrots! They are also the leading *source* of beta carotene. Add to that the high content of flavonoids, and you have a very hard-working vegetable that fights cancer, heart disease, and degenerative eye disease. Besides that, carrots are a great snack to take to the movies—crunchy, sweet, and guiltless.

This celebrant of spring is a root vegetable. Carrots are the most beguiling of all the vegetables to me. The best part of a carrot grows where no one can admire it. It is tucked away in a womb of soil, in a solitary place of becoming. For the entire growing season, green leaves on long stalks are the only thing showing above ground, giving no hint of the vegetable that's taking shape below. Only a God of intentional design would put a big orange thing under the ground while allowing lacelike leaves to stand on stage. Redemption has more than once surprised us by bringing life from unexpected places, light from dark spaces. Children are little root vegetables too. For nine months they develop in seclusion and darkness before emerging all pink and lovely. As they age, character, knowledge, personality, and life continue to germinate inside them until one day these little ones ripen into young adults. The important things that were planted in the unseen places of their souls burst forth in startling color.

The investment of time and faithfulness by those who tend the young ones is rewarded with muddy hands, calluses, and, eventually, beautiful fruit.

Jamie is in charge of what happens with the young "root vegetables" at the Village Chapel. She creatively directs the programming for our crop of babies, preschoolers, and school-age children, introducing them to the God who lovingly created them. After seeing Jamie transform the bland and moldy office space we started with into a delightful room filled with color and wonder that the children don't want to leave, I am convinced that she has the ability to see life where there was none, the perfect talent for nurturing root vegetables.

This year's first spring potluck was on a Sunday, when the crocuses were bravely standing against a persistent cold, and we were all hovering near the heat ducts. The tables served up spring soups and some light casseroles, along with Cristin and Kale's Spring Rolls—a translucent layer of rice paper chock-full of carrots, peppers, and bok choy. And Jamie brought a bowl full of carrot muffins. The bite-sized muffins had the perfect spring mix of pineapple and carrots, with the lingering winter flavors of cinnamon, cloves, and maple syrup. They were reflective of the season past, indicative of the season to come.

The moist texture of the muffins was mostly owing to the five cups of carrot pulp in the recipe. Jamie makes carrot juice every morning, and it nets her mounds of pulp that she can never bring herself to throw away. So she put the weeks' allotment of carrot pulp into muffins, and I ate a fistful of the result.

Spring invites the lesson of the root vegetable. The picture of goodness unearthed from darkness is reminiscent of resurrection, redemption, and rescue. So when the temperatures begin to rise, I go out to my garden to plow it up, rake it, and resow it, planting the possibility of new life in its dark places, hoping to reconstitute the promises that grow even in the dark.

# CRISTIN AND KALE'S SPRING ROLLS

*1 cucumber, peeled (approximately 3 inches long)*
*2 carrots, peeled*
*1 red bell pepper*
*2 stalks bok choy*
*2 ounces rice sticks (thin, clear Asian noodles)*
*15–20 fresh cilantro leaves, chopped*
*15–20 fresh mint leaves, chopped*
*8 sheets of rice paper*
*sweet-and-sour sauce, to serve*

Soak rice sticks in hot water about 30 minutes to soften. Slice cucumber, carrots, red pepper, and bok choy into 1/8-inch-wide pieces. Cook rice sticks in boiling water 1 minute. Drain and toss with vegetables, cilantro, and mint. Soak rice paper in hot water for 1–2 minutes to soften. Place small handful of vegetable mixture on bottom third of each sheet of rice paper. Fold ends in and tightly roll up each sheet of rice paper. Cut each roll in half on an angle. Serve with sweet-and-sour sauce.

*Note:* You can usually find rice sticks and rice paper in the Asian food section of your grocery store.

# JAMIE'S CARROT MUFFINS

6 cups whole-wheat flour

4 teaspoons baking soda

1 teaspoon baking powder

2 teaspoons ground cinnamon

2 teaspoons ground cloves

2 teaspoons salt

1 cup butter, softened

1 1/2 cups real maple syrup

1 1/2 cups unsweetened applesauce

5 cups carrot pulp (from what is left over after juicing carrots)

1 1/2 cups chopped pecans or walnuts

1 can unsweetened, crushed pineapple, drained
     (reserve juice)

Preheat oven to 350 degrees. In large mixing bowl, mix dry
ingredients. Add butter, syrup, applesauce, carrot pulp, nuts,
and pineapple. Combine thoroughly. If mixture is too dry, use
pineapple juice to moisten. Pour into greased muffin pans and
bake about 30 minutes or until toothpick inserted comes out dry.

# CAFETERIA POTLUCK

*Choosing and Being Found Chosen*

I was mostly a "bringer" in my school years. I sat quietly at a table with my sack lunch, observing the herds of my peers collected around long, shadowy tables. The memories of my cafeteria experience fill me with more angst than awe, as I recall the loneliness of feeling unchosen.

My family moved in October of my fourth-grade year. I became a student in Mrs. Salzman's class more than a month after school had begun, and Taylor Elementary in Arlington, Virginia, became my fourth academic home in four years.

I didn't so much mind the moving. After a while, in fact, I took advantage of the opportunity to re-create myself with each new address. At 5263 D Street in Memphis, Tennessee, I was Bookworm Library Girl. In Charleston, South Carolina, I went for the athletic persona, playing baseball with the boys and collecting my first shiner. I would be class clown, storyteller, artist, honor student, and teacher's pet all before I hit junior high.

Fourth grade and the house on Upshur Street in Virginia saw me initiate the Eccentric Quirky Girl persona, to which I would return most often and most comfortably over the years. These seasons found me walking or swinging alone on the playground, experimenting with asymmetric hairstyles, and preferring my imagination and its version of my world to the homogenous realm of reality.

The first day in Mrs. Salzman's class, I was assigned to sit at a cluster of desks with some other students, mostly girls. Perhaps there were boys, too, but they weren't yet in full possession of their verbal skills, so I do not have a distinct memory of any interaction with them. The girls were more verbally advanced at this age, while the boys ruled on the playground with motor skills and the occasional utterance of "No way!" "It was foul!" and sometimes, "You cheat!"

Mrs. Salzman escorted me over to the small group of students, introduced me, left me, and made her way to the chalkboard. I stood there clutching my shiny, new red patent-leather binder and pencil bag to my chest. Uncomfortable silence. Awkward throat clearing. Averted gazes and unself-conscious, bored yawns.

Finally, one of the girls rolled her eyes my way and through an Elvis-curled lip said, "Are you weird?" Not that I am still bitter in any way over this experience, but her name was Jessica, and I do feel a little sick to my stomach right now.

I said, "Yes." And this was the beginning of a long and isolated season in my scholastic career.

As Weird Girl, I spent most of my lunches sitting alone. Occasionally I would reintroduce Library Girl and read a book with my lunch. Then I would become Weird Library Girl. This did not enhance my prospects for company at the cafeteria table, which was okay with me for the most part. But it did mean that I missed out on trading food, sampling other mothers' sandwiches, and experimenting outside the realm of my own lunchbox.

The actual sitting and eating alone was not an issue. Once I was seated at a table, the worst part of the cafeteria experience was over. The real trauma I faced every day started a few steps before that. I would set my Barbie lunchbox on the blue, industrial plastic tray, make my way through the line to collect my pint of vitamin-D homogenized milk, and move along with the herd to the checkout lady. After handing the woman in the white polyester dress, white stockings, and black hairnet my coins, life in the school cafeteria would move in slow motion as I made the ninety-degree turn to face the jury of my peers.

If an illustrated pop-up had emerged from my head as I looked out into the crowd, it would have shown pictures of snapping alligators, and lions pawing the dirt, and hissing snakes slithering along the ground. But those menacing images didn't appear when we picked kids to be on kickball or dodge-ball teams. I was quite confident in those realms and found myself picked quickly. But in the cafeteria my skills were less valued, and I remained mostly unpicked. I looked out on the vast horizon of elementary children, scanning for an upraised hand waving me over, listening for an invitation of "Come sit with me." If only someone remembered my dodge-ball abilities, my shape-shifting skills, my vast knowledge of Nancy Drew books. Surely then I would be chosen.

Lonely Lunch Girl made other appearances in my life, but fortunately I moved again the summer before sixth grade and left her at Taylor Elementary for a season. I don't know whether I was able to smooth out some of my eccentric edges that summer or whether Beech Tree Elementary just imported more quirky children so that I naturally fit in better. I do know that my cafeteria memories from that time have more names and faces, and I have distinct memories of Paula Jones's mom's meatloaf sandwiches. (As I conjure up that flavor in my mind, I remember learning that "the grass isn't always greener.")

The cafeteria potluck is about more than swapping what our moms put in our lunchboxes. Community meals present the opportunity to be "picked." Whether in a cafeteria, a gymnasium, or an old chapel, they are about being chosen to sit with and talk with. They are about taking home an empty dish with the sides scraped clean because your dish was chosen. They are about someone acknowledging your existence, knowing your name, validating your presence.

Perhaps now that I am older, I see that cafeteria potlucks are also about *choosing*. I have the power to empty a bowl, fill a table, and welcome the "weird girl." A lifetime of personas cannot warm the chair beside me, and waiting to be chosen may mean eating alone. It takes courage to switch from feeling sorry for myself, as I mourn my not being chosen, to inviting someone else to sit with me. But if I can let go of my own discomfort, I'm freed to see that someone else is waiting to be chosen too and that belonging is a gift I can give as well as receive.

## CAFETERIA SPAGHETTI

*1 pound lean ground beef*
*1 jar prepared spaghetti sauce*
*1 (1-pound) box of spaghetti pasta*

Brown ground beef. Add spaghetti sauce and simmer. Boil pasta
and drain. Plate the spaghetti and top with sauce. Serve with dry,
stale Texas toast.

*Note:* To take this from the cafeteria to the dining room, use vermicelli instead of spaghetti, and grate fresh parmesan cheese on
top. Sometimes, instead of meat sauce, I heat diced Italian stewed
tomatoes and serve them over the vermicelli. This is a fresh and
light alternative for last-minute meals. I keep several cans of
stewed tomatoes and a couple of boxes of pasta in the pantry all
the time, in case people drop by.

# SOUP POTLUCK

*Seasoned by One Another*

F all finds us bringing out the six-outlet power strip at the Village Chapel and lining the outer walls with places to plug in slow cookers. We invite the potluckers to bring their favorite soup, stew, chili, borscht, goulash, or potage. Some dishes are made from a specific recipe; others are pragmatic collections of refrigerator leftovers held together by a broth of some sort. Light herb-seasoned salads and vegetables are replaced by exotic and smoky spices, and deviled-egg platters retire in deference to stockpots and heavy skillets. With cityscape piles of Styrofoam bowls on the ends of serving tables, Soup Supper Season is officially open.

Soup making is a distinct category of cooking and calls for the ability to see the big-picture flavor through a collection of smaller flavors. A good soup maker can take something that was designed to be served one way and repackage it in the company of new and unrelated foods in a stockpot. Finding a way to unify and harmonize the ingredients in an

appropriate broth is the final step that makes the miscella-
neous items "soup."

My need for soup skills sends me to my sister. Melani
undoubtedly makes the best homemade vegetable soup I
have ever eaten. Fearless with seasoning yet discriminating in
taste, she has the highly refined instincts of a soup chemist.
But Melani's gifts of nurturing go beyond soups to caring
conversation and wise insight. On many occasions since
Mom died, the sound of Melani's voice has been home for
me. Countless times she has reminded me to take care of
myself, allow some room in my cramped schedule, and relax
a little on the overachieving. When time spent with people
begins to drain my reserves, she tells me to use two words
more often: "Hmm…" and "Oh…." (These words indicate
that you care, but they don't invite more details.) Melani is
my big sister, and she gathers me up when I'm in pieces and
carries me to higher ground. She does that for Dad, too, and
for everyone she encounters. It feels a lot like Mom.

One of the secrets to Melani's soup making is that she
has a treasure-trove of leftovers in her refrigerator with which
to seed the pot. First, she lays a flavor foundation with homemade stock made from a boiled chicken or turkey carcass,
seasoning the water with salt and pepper. Next, she browns
ground beef with garlic and onions and adds stewed tomatoes. Then she starts the well-choreographed emptying of the
refrigerator: leftovers of corn, green beans, squash, and limas
mingle with her careful combination of chili powder and

cumin, taco seasoning and dried herbs. Black-eyed peas some-times make an appearance—and all of it tastes best reheated in the microwave in a coffee mug just before bed. Last fall I even found myself refusing Blue Bell Ice Cream in favor of a third bowl of soup.

One Christmas, at the end of a week of holiday cooking, Melani started a soup by boiling what looked to me like a used-up hambone. Evidently there was still something worth saving on it, though—a good soup maker has eyes for sal-vaging food. Melani added a little bag of dried green peas, and that night we dined on a rich and thick split-pea soup. It took the chill off and kept it off for the rest of the night.

I had never made soup before, so when I approached the stockpot at the start of Soup Supper Season, I prayed for a little of my sister to manifest itself in me. (I would love to be more like Melani in most ways, but at that point I would have settled for her soup instincts.) I decided that a day of experimentation was in order before the night of the first potluck, so I looked through my refrigerator in search of left-overs I might be able to introduce to one another. With all the flavors in such close quarters, it would be important for them to be amiable. As Jim and I never have leftovers in our refrigerator, though, and there is rarely a hambone in reach, I was at a distinct disadvantage. So with the courage of my sisterly heritage, I struck out in a slightly different direction for my first foray into soup making.

At my neighborhood market, I was introduced to the

joys of ready-made chicken stock. This discovery eliminated the unpleasant and time-consuming process of boiling the chicken or turkey carcass, and I moved on to confront the lack-of-leftovers issue. In the midst of my ever-progressing soup revelation, I remembered that leftovers start out as "first servings," so I harvested vegetables from the produce section that I could cook up and simply *pretend* were leftovers. My basket full, I checked out and drove home, still concerned about my potential for soup success.

The three phone calls to my sister that day brought needed reassurance that I could pull off this task. During the fourth phone call, Melani started answering me with "Oh…" and "Hmm…." I got the message. I would have to brave this soup-making journey on my own at some point, and that time had come.

A few sautéed-and-simmered hours later, my stockpot was filled to the brim. Zucchini and yellow squash, frozen shoe-peg corn, diced potatoes, spicy V8 juice, RoTel Mexican stewed tomatoes, a small can of tomato paste, and four cans of chicken stock scented my kitchen with smells reminiscent of my sister's home. They were now becoming my own scents, and my excitement was building. I served up the soup in a wide bowl with corn bread baked in a cast-iron frying pan, and I held my breath before Jim and I took the first bite. Each of the flavors had carried their responsibility well, and the sum of the parts equaled much more than the individual ingredients. I called my sister.

Later that week, after the flavors of the soup had mingled and mellowed to perfection, I took it to our first Soup Supper Potluck. Huddled around the savory scents from the potluck tables that cool fall evening, we found ourselves enjoying the simplicity of meal-in-a-bowl eating. Leftovers turned into soups of plenty as chilis with and without meat, dumplings, stews, and porridge all bubbled next to one another in beckoning bulk. The influence of other sisters was evident in other pots on the table, and other family recipes filled our bowls with nurturing flavor.

"We should get small cups to serve the soup in," Ben suggested, "to make it easier for people to sample a variety of flavors instead of using just one big bowl of one soup."

I'm still working on that good idea, searching for soup-sampler-sized bowls.

Looking over the seated hall, I realized what a perfect analogy soup is for community. The gathering of families and singles; the recently married, the not-so-recently married, and the recently *un*married; the professionals and non-professionals; the children and the grownups all looked suspiciously like a pot of soup.

At one table, for example, I saw my friend Margaret, who brought her thirteen-year-old neighbor Caroline. Margaret is gifted at motivating and encouraging people, and Caroline blooms in her presence. Seated with them were Dan and June, a fifty-something couple married for more than twenty years. Dan had a record deal in the 1970s and now builds houses. He encourages the young musicians at the Village Chapel and continues to write songs as well. June works at a high school and mentors a young neighbor, reading books with her and talking about her life, interested in what interests her. A thirty-something couple sat across the table. They had been married to each other at one time and then divorced and are now trying to find their way back to each other. Jacinda sat next to them. Soft spoken and gentle spirited, she is in her twenties, recently back from teaching English to the poor of Indonesia. Tony, usually busy with setting up the sound equipment, took a moment to sit and eat with the others at the table. He is recently divorced and mending from the pain of disappointment. A gifted professional sound engineer for MTV, he serves the Chapel whenever the doors are open. All of these people shared a table, all of them flavored one anothers' lives with their stories.

A collection of unrelated ingredients that come together to flavor one another in a unifying broth describes a soup— and it describes the best of what happens at our potlucks. Some of us come feeling overcooked or leftover, underflavored or indistinct, strong, fresh, or tired. But in the context of the whole, we are a soup, seasoned by one another, bringing out the best of what each has to offer.

## MELANI'S TACO-VEGETABLE SOUP

*1 pound lean ground beef*
*1/2 white or yellow onion, chopped*
*1 can corn, undrained*
*1 can diced tomatoes, undrained*
*1 can RoTel tomatoes, undrained*
*1 can pinto beans, undrained*
*1 packet taco seasoning mix*
*1 packet ranch dressing mix*
*2 cups water*

Brown ground beef and onion together in stockpot. Add other ingredients. Simmer slowly 2–3 hours.

*Note:* Try adding cooked rice or chopped greens to the soup for added texture or color. The soup can also be topped with any combination of shredded cheese, diced jalapeños, chopped red onion, or cool slices of avocado. Try a dollop of sour cream to cool the heat. By the way, no carcass boiling is necessary to build the stock for this soup.

## KIM'S COCONUT-CURRY SHRIMP SOUP

*5 red potatoes, cubed*
*2 tablespoons vegetable oil*
*1 stalk celery, diced*
*2 tablespoons curry powder*
*1 bag frozen medium shrimp, thawed, peeled, deveined,*
   *tails removed*
*2 (14 1/2-ounce) cans fat-free chicken broth*
*1 (14-ounce) can unsweetened coconut milk*
*freshly squeezed juice of one large lime*
*1/2 cup chopped fresh cilantro*
*2 stalks lemon grass*

In medium pot, boil potatoes until tender crisp. Drain. Heat oil in large stockpot over medium heat. Add celery, potatoes, and curry powder. Cook until celery is softened and flavors have had a chance to mingle. Add defrosted shrimp, chicken broth, coconut milk, lime juice, cilantro, and lemon grass. Simmer soup 1 hour. Remove lemon grass before serving.

*Note:* If I have time, I use a slow cooker and cook 3 hours on high. Then I can plug the cooker in at the potluck and the soup stays warm.

# CAKE POTLUCK

## *Creativity Is a Gift*

More than a dozen years ago, when we found out that Evy, pronounced like "Chevy," was pregnant with her baby girl, Miró, Deb and I wanted to plan a shower to honor the occasion. The three of us had become a "tripod" of friends, lovingly interdependent.

While successful at some showers, games like Diaper the Baby Doll or Bottle Bowling were not going to fly at this gathering. We needed something that was specific to Evy, something that honored the distinctive person she is. After brainstorming for an afternoon, Deb and I came up with the plan to host a cake-potluck baby shower. We could think of no better way to celebrate Evy than to encourage her friends to create something in her honor.

When I met Evy, she had bright red hair cut very short and styled all sticky-outy. One of the first things I noticed about her was how easily she laughed. When humored, she would throw her head back like a PEZ dispenser and shoot laughter out like pellets of candy. She drove a white VW convertible, and at the time, she and her husband, Jerry, had only one child, a son named Miles. They lived in a duplex where Evy had appropriated the living room as a bedroom, the dining room as a living room, and the biggest room as the entry hall. The first time Jim and I went to their house, we gathered on a church pew that served as their couch, watched rodeo, and ate Bananas Foster. Living outside of the typically expected, capturing possibility, and creating more out of less is Evy's way of being.

The VW that distinguished Evy and Jerry on the Nashville roads became our buggy of transport on Saturday mornings. Driving from yard sale to yard sale, Evy and I put the top down on the car and breathed in the potential of a morning of junk hunting. We loaded items that had been overlooked by most buyers into the back of the VW, taking home rusted lamps, paint-stripped furniture, cobwebbed frames, and old draperies for imminent makeovers. Even the lamest of yard sales usually netted Evy a one-of-a-kind treasure. Now, several years later, she is a first-call interior designer with more work than she can keep up with. I can't help but think that the yard sales had been a proving ground for her designer's eye, honing her talent for seeing and assembling exceptional environments.

Evy was always the first one to find the quirky little restaurants in town. She introduced us to Thai, Vietnamese, Indian, Cuban, Moroccan, and Mexican restaurants that would have gone unnoticed by the untrained eye. We sat across from each other at hundreds of tables during our thirties, squeezing the bigness out of small restaurants and unusual flavors. At Deb's fortieth birthday party, Evy and I stepped out of the kitchen of our favorite Indian restaurant in vintage evening gowns and cat-eye glasses, playing "Happy Birthday" on accordions.

The cake-potluck baby shower grew with our enthusiasm. More than sixty names on our invite list begged for a venue larger than a living room, so we moved the event to Evy's interior-design shop. An old building in a historic section of town, the shop has aged hardwood floors and rooms full of antiques and persian rugs, lush upholstered divans from the fifties, and elegant french armoires under sparkling crystal chandeliers. We rented china and silver for the evening and served coffee from bright chrome urns.

One of the best things about a potluck is that it approximates family in community. Kinship is lovingly kneaded into shared experience and common interest, creating an environment ripe for belonging. In an unselfconscious way, the potluck converts strangers and acquaintances into what begins to feel like chosen family. That night the family was large, and we were inspired by the large-hearted creativity that Evy always gave us. And so we created cakes in celebration of the newly expected member of the family.

In the early evening the fall sun faded graciously. The candles and dim chandeliers gave the room a warm glow.

Before the first candle dripped, the friends began to come, bearing stacked, baked, iced, glazed, and powdered cakes of all shapes and flavors. Michelle brought a bright fruit tart in a scalloped buttery crust. Her husband, Jimmy, made a strawberry shortcake with frosting as light and tasty as strawberry air. Deb prepared a beautiful chocolate-date torte. My Jim made Ugly Chocolate Cake, and I assembled Hummingbird Cake for the occasion. All the potluckers, whether or not they thought of themselves as endowed with creative gifts, produced something of loving delight. Fearless expressions of sugar and flour covered the antique tabletops. We all wanted to honor the baby of the little redhead who loved life lived in its most creative expression. Every time I saw her throughout the evening, my friend was balancing a plate with a different sliver of cake on her protruding eight-month-pregnant belly and leading a small group of friends in something that ended in laughter.

The creative expressions of love spilled from the potluck cake table to the gift table, where the presents for baby Miró were lovely creations of handsewn baby clothes and blankets, small paintings in delicate frames, original poems, and handmade cards.

It struck me that night that creativity is not as complicated or mysterious as its romantic persona would have us believe. It shows itself in the handiwork of a mother of five who finds a new way to make a baloney sandwich, or in the way an office employee arranges her desk with a flair for efficiency. It is found in the person sitting in traffic who finds an alternate route, in the preschool teacher who motivates five-year-olds, in the painter or writer who faces an empty page and turns it into art, and in the friend who bakes a cake as a gift of celebration.

Our cake potluck was a reminder that the fullness of life is often experienced in simple everyday things. Like homemade cakes and a new baby girl. The cakes we created not only celebrated baby Miró but also drew us close to God. Not so much because of the sugar or the butter or the flour, but because we closely reflect our Maker's heart when we create. That was his first act—"in the beginning God created." Since we were created in his image, our attempts at creating are a natural expression, a lovely privilege that can seize us from soulful poverty, from ho-hum living, or the apathy of life without wonder and beauty.

That's how Evy lives, in constant pursuit of creative possibilities, eliminating remnants of lazy and mediocre days. In the company of chosen family.

# DEB'S CHOCOLATE-DATE TORTE

*1 (8-ounce) bag almonds, unpeeled*
*1 (8-ounce) block semisweet cooking chocolate*
*6 egg whites*
*1/2 cup superfine castor sugar (If you can't find any, you*
    *can make your own by grinding granulated sugar in*
    *a food processor for a few minutes.)*
*1 (8-ounce) container dates, finely chopped*
*whipped cream*
*nuts, grated chocolate, or berries, for garnish*

Preheat oven to 350 degrees. Grease a round 8-inch baking pan
and line with parchment. Place almonds and chocolate in
blender or food processor and chop into fine bits. In separate
bowl, beat egg whites until they form stiff peaks, and then gradu-
ally add castor sugar. Fold in almonds, chocolate, and dates. Pour
into prepared baking pan. Bake 45 minutes.

At end of baking time, turn off oven and open door slightly
to allow torte to cool. When torte is cool, remove from oven,
turn onto serving platter, and refrigerate overnight.

To serve, spread top with whipped cream and garnish with
nuts, grated chocolate, or berries. (Serves 8–10.)

*Note:* This torte is crumbly and is best cut when refrigerated. It
will keep in the refrigerator for several days.

## AUNT GENE'S HUMMINGBIRD CAKE

3 cups all-purpose flour

2 cups granulated sugar

1 teaspoon baking soda

1 teaspoon ground cinnamon

1 teaspoon salt

2 eggs, beaten

1 cup vegetable oil

1 1/2 teaspoons vanilla extract

1 (8-ounce) can crushed pineapple, undrained

1 cup chopped pecans

2 cups chopped bananas

Preheat oven to 350 degrees. Combine first 5 ingredients in large bowl. Add eggs and oil. Stir until dry ingredients are moistened. (Do not beat!) Add vanilla extract and fold in remaining ingredients. Spoon batter into 3 greased and floured 9-inch cake pans. Bake 25–30 minutes or until toothpick inserted in middle comes out clean.

Cool in pans 10 minutes. Remove cake from pans and cool completely before frosting.

### Cream-Cheese Frosting

1 (8-ounce) package cream cheese

1/2 cup butter, softened

*1 (16-ounce) package powdered sugar, sifted*
*1 teaspoon vanilla*
*1/2 cup chopped pecans*

Cream the cream cheese and butter until smooth. Add sugar and vanilla. Beat until light and fluffy. Spread frosting on top of first layer of cake, then top with second layer and finish frosting on top and sides. Cover cake with chopped pecans.

# DAD'S DESSERT POTLUCK

*Reentering Community*

Jim asked me last night, "When is the last time you laughed until milk came out your nose?"

It was an unexpected question, and I had to pause and think.

"Does Diet Coke count?" I finally responded. "Because if Diet Coke coming out your nose counts, then it was last week when I talked to Dad."

It's ironic that the times I have laughed the hardest lately have been while talking on the phone with my dad. We lost Mom to lung cancer less than two years ago, and laughter is only recently returning to our emotional vocabulary. It just seemed that there wasn't as much to laugh about without her, and though I know she would want us to have deep laughter in our lives, it has taken us awhile to find it again.

My dad, my sister, and I live in different states. The distance has been hard, but we have logged a lot of telephone hours, sharing our lives in detailed conversations. We share the simple stories of how we pass our days, what things we are working on, how we are coping with the new season without Mom, and how much the three of us miss one another in Orlando, Nashville, and Houston.

We try to pick up on one another's rhythms and routines and join in from afar. On evenings when Jim and I are going to meet Jodi and Brad for dinner, Dad will call and say, "I know it's Taco Tuesday. Order me an enchilada!"

Dad goes to dinner at church on Wednesday nights, so I call and ask him to eat some pie for me. If we haven't spoken to Dad in a few days, my sister and I confer like worried hens. Careful not to smother him, we call just to "check in," to take his emotional pulse and love him through the phone.

The first hint of laughter returning after Mom died leaked out the time Dad called to announce, "I guess it isn't okay to put liquid dish soap in the dishwasher." He had filled the main cup inside the dishwasher door with Palmolive, and he even filled the other cup, which is usually used for a drying agent. Pleased with his efficiency, he shut the dishwasher, started the cycle, and went to bed.

The entire kitchen floor was ankle deep in bubbles when he went in to make his coffee in the morning. The mess was almost worth the laughter it brought, and I was grateful he wasn't angry with himself, that he was finding a way to laugh through this new learning curve of domestic skills. At the same time, I was concerned, because he had to use most of the towels in the house to soak up the suds, and now he would have to use the washing machine.

Before we hung up, we went over the dishwasher rules and clarified the distinction between dish soap and dishwasher soap. Neither milk nor Diet Coke came out of my nose during that conversation, but that was only because I wasn't drinking any at the time.

Melani coached Dad on washing-machine usage, and he has had minimal shrinking, bleeding, or oversudsing in that department. He is naturally gifted with a sponge and a vacuum and has since mastered the responsibilities of keeping the house. But it is a big change for him, and I wish once in a while I could just drop in and dust, or fold some sheets, or Windex a few windows. I would like to sit with him on his screened-in porch and watch the Florida sun slide below the ninth hole behind his house in the early evening.

So Dad is finding out who he is as a single man in his seventies. Mom was a traditional wife of her era. She tended to the house, paid the bills, and always had a hot meal ready for Dad when he got home from the office. She was also the driving force in their social world, and that has left its own emptiness. Her natural charm made everyone her friend, and she had a way of encouraging anyone she came in contact with. People wanted to be with Mom.

The drastic change to Dad's everyday schedule makes my breath catch in my throat when I think about it. As much as I want to rescue him from the pain, I know there is only one way out for him, and that is *through* it. One step following another, until one day the ache isn't as bad and there are friends to call, people to visit.

Dad eats out often, but when he eats at home, he has perfected the art of vegetable steaming and toaster-oven cooking. If it won't fit in the electric steamer or the toaster oven, he doesn't need to eat it. Ice cream is still his favorite meal of the day, and he has been known to put coffee on his cereal if there is no milk in the house. His creative efforts keep us laughing and ease the sadness, but Mom's absence is still underlined in each story, particularly the stories about food.

After Mom's death, Dad stayed in the house they lived in, with her scent, her touch, her memory everywhere. I don't know how he was able to do it. Over time, he has made some changes and taken the opportunity to reinterpret the house to fit his own style. The bedroom got new linens and curtains and a jungle-themed print for the wall. He added a sunroom on the back of the house and rearranged, repainted, and reclaimed each room. It seemed that now he was ready to invite people in.

I was so pleased when Dad spoke one week about hosting his Thursday night men's Bible study. It would be the first entertaining he had done since Mom died, and I was proud of his courage to take more first steps.

I asked him the week before what he might serve his

group. He said the guys were all bringing a little something and that he hadn't given it much thought, but perhaps he would serve dessert. Potluck dessert was a perfect first way to entertain. Pushing a little, I made some suggestions and joked with him about what he might make in the toaster oven. But if my dad knows anything about food, he knows his desserts, and I was confident he would come up with something the men would enjoy.

The next week Dad called me from one of his morning walks to report in on the menu. He had been to several places looking for inspiring desserts, and he finally settled on a pre-made giant cookie/ice-cream sandwich from the grocery store. I smiled into the telephone seven hundred miles away and thought it would be a memorable potluck. Out of his loneliness, Dad would give, and it would be about more than ice cream and a big cookie. This was Dad's party to host, his welcome to extend.

The morning of his men's gathering, he called. He had just gotten back from his walk and was disturbed to find that the cookie dessert he had taken out of the freezer two hours earlier—so it would be ready for that night—was now mush.

This was the conversation that provoked the Diet Coke from the nose I mentioned earlier. I pictured the soggy cookie dessert and Dad's impish grin as he looked at it in the kitchen while we discussed the challenge a frozen dessert presents when you have to cut it without defrosting it. I prayed for the men who would eat it that night, since Dad had spoken with the store, and they told him to simply refreeze the dessert and take it out fifteen minutes before serving. I thought how sad it would be for the men to end up in the ER with botulism after Dad's first potluck. But mostly I was proud of Dad for trying new things and laughing at himself. I laughed too.

I suppose that there wasn't much about this social gathering that looked like the ones Dad had enjoyed with Mom. But then, everything is different now, and Dad is courageously finding his way. The table linens were familiar to him, the bright place mats and napkins Mom used to entertain with. I thought of the many times she had washed and folded the napkins, patting each crease. Dad probably did not pat them, but they were folded and ready, freshly clean after his successful use of the washing machine. Available for a new start.

If you had to pick a way to begin to breathe again after the loss of your mate of over fifty years, you might as well pick a dessert potluck. Inviting people into your home is like inviting them into your life, your heart. Dad was ready, and I know he welcomed each of the men with a smile and a hand on their shoulders.

He told me later that nobody commented on the dessert but that they were enjoying one another's company so much, they didn't get up from the table all night. I rather doubt there was much talk of recipes, but I'm sure a lot of stories were shared. And I would guess that it was a stretch for Dad to expose his heart, to risk vulnerability in his newly single status. Having a mate gives you a safety zone, a verbal support that frees you to participate in community in a fearless way. Mom gave Dad "cover," and all he had to do in these settings was smile at her, relaxed in the company of his soul mate. But that night he flew solo for the first time in more than fifty years. As is true with every potluck I have experienced, it was in giving that Dad found himself belonging.

After all his guests left, Dad cleaned up and put away the leftovers. He wiped down the countertops, shining them as Mom would have, and tucked the dishes into the dishwasher. He filled the little cup with powdered dishwasher detergent, shut the door, and started the wash cycle.

## FROZEN-COOKIE DESSERT PIE
## (INSTEAD OF A GIANT GROCERY-STORE-COOKIE ICE-CREAM SANDWICH)

*2 cups crushed cookies*
*1 stick butter, melted*
*1/2 gallon ice cream or frozen yogurt*

Mix crushed cookies and melted butter and press into bottom and sides of greased 9-inch pie pan. Put pan in freezer for 1/2 hour or so to harden, and remove ice cream or frozen yogurt from freezer to soften. Remove pan from freezer and spread ice cream or frozen yogurt over crust. Cover tightly with foil and freeze firm. (This pie fits in the freezer a little easier than those giant premade cookie desserts.) Serve in slices.

*Variations:* This recipe can be made with sugar-free or dairy-free ingredients. You can also choose any combination of cookies, ice cream, yogurt, or toppings for this dessert. Here are a few suggestions:

- Oreos and vanilla ice cream, drizzled with chocolate syrup
- shortbread cookies and strawberry frozen yogurt, topped with fresh strawberries
- peanut-butter cookies with chocolate ice cream, sprinkled with peanuts and drizzled with chocolate syrup

# INVITATIONS

*Responding to the Call of Welcome*

I f it is Halloween, there will be an "e-vite" in my in-box. Stephen and Lauri will send the Internet invitation, requesting that we attend their potluck cookout and bring something to put on the grill. No stamps to lick, no envelopes to address, no phone calls to make with this efficient welcome. The e-vite shows the list of people who are invited and gives them a place to RSVP, displaying their response for all to read. Jim and I respond yes to our Halloween e-vites whenever we can.

The invitation respectfully requests that we wear costumes, and I fret for weeks over finding something that will allow my husband, the pastor, to maintain his dignity. He would be thrilled to dress as Spider-Man. Perhaps I am the only one concerned about his dignity.

In this "music city," Stephen is a producer, so good music is always playing at Stephen and Lauri's house. A lovely mix of the Beatles, Patty Griffin, and a new band or two that

Stephen works with plays softly through the speakers set outside for the occasion. We lean into the rhythm of a lazy fall schedule and choose from the bowls of baked beans; the plates of burgers, hot dogs, and chicken; and the baskets of other communal offerings ranging from grilled vegetables to Reed and Dianne's Cabbage Slaw.

We stay outdoors to eat Lauri's Berry Brownie Torte at the end of the evening, even though the coolness of fall has begun to claim any remnants of summer warmth. White sparkle lights line the spines of the umbrella over the table, and citronella candles scent the October air, repelling the unwelcome mosquitoes that linger.

Lauri's hot cider and the self-serve caramel apples are two of this Halloween potluck's staples. The cider is a warming mix of cinnamon and spices, and the caramel is a sweet and sticky puddle waiting for apples to be dunked in it. I dip only a slice or two of apple, though I would like to sit in a corner with the caramel and apples and eat all of them. Instead, I continue to make conversation with an unusual but charming girl in a white wig. She has a whoopee cushion in the purse hanging from her shoulder, and whenever she greets new arrivals, she puts out her hand to shake theirs and at the same time gives her purse a squeeze. Sometimes people laugh. Jim laughs every time.

These gatherings are relaxed evenings of connection. We talk about the impending holiday season and the various joys and frustrations of dysfunctional family gatherings, and I struggle to take any of the conversation seriously as I look at the earnest faces of adults dressed as gypsies, belly dancers, mermaids, baseball players, pirates, and punk rockers. But we are present to the moment, a moment that begins when Stephen and Lauri first send the e-vite and ends only when the last Beatles song of the evening has finished playing.

Another invitation regularly marks the calendar at our home. On the third week of every month, paper invitations appear in the mailbox hanging on our front porch. Actual licked-stamp envelopes appear like little gifts waiting to be ripped open. It is an entirely different experience from receiving an e-vite, but the welcome is the same. Sometimes the stamped invites are enclosed in legal envelopes with crooked white labels, or in neatly computer-addressed envelopes, or sometimes our name is hand scrawled across the envelope like people used to do in the latter part of the twentieth century. However the envelopes are addressed, the host home for that month's Supper Club sends the information, directing us to come to their house on a particular Friday night. Once, when the invitation came from Celia, I was distracted by thoughts of her Poppy-Seed Chicken as I tore open her envelope. If I had been paying attention, I would have remembered that she was teaching elementary school that year, and I might have caught the confetti before it flew all over my kitchen floor. (That was last fall, and this summer I found a piece of confetti stuck to the bottom of our dog Rose's paw.)

These paper invitations are from the Supper Club of the

First Presbyterian Sunday-school class where Jim has been the guest speaker for almost five years. Unlike Stephen and Lauri, few of us are well versed in the ways of e-viting. I was the most computer savvy and sent out e-mail invitations when we hosted the Supper Club at our house. They weren't fancy like e-vites, just the essential information in an e-mail. Then I proceeded to call everyone anyway in case the Internet had ceased to function in Nashville that morning.

The people in the Supper Club do not require that you show your invitation at the door, as we are a simple group of about twenty who all know one another. We know one another because we have potlucked together once a month for five years. That's sixty paper invitations that have come to my mailbox and hung on my refrigerator. Sixty gatherings that have seen the group through sicknesses, career changes, suspicious lumps, aging parents, growing children, family vacations, and even the death of loved ones. Sixty potlucks that have forged bonds that began on the front of an envelope five years ago.

I hear about John and his daughter winning the squirrel hunt at a lodge and about Chuck's new season as a grad student. I learn about planting bulbs from Susan and about the equestrian world from Dibbie. I talk to Eric and Anne about remodeling their lovely Tudor home, and Mickey evangelizes about the Fab Four, a Beatles tribute band. Conversations flow like a needle and thread, reconnecting us to one anothers' lives. It feels so much like potlucks when I was growing up that I look in the kitchen and can almost see my aunts hovering at the sink.

Sometimes it's easier to talk about the appetizers, football, or the dog's new tricks even though someone in the group is hurting, grieving, or sad. Last month Gordon and I talked about the football game for a while, but eventually we talked about his dad. He told me how hard it was to watch him struggle with cancer, sick and diminished, a frail reflection of the bigger-than-life dad Gordon has always known. At this month's Supper Club, we will talk about the funeral and how lovely it was that so many came.

I know all of these things because I get an invitation the third week of the month, every month, inviting me into these people's lives. I love the welcome that invitations signal. Whether they are e-vites, paper invitations, or silent invitations, they speak our names and whisper that we have been chosen.

As God spoke creation into being, his first invitation was verbal: "Let there be…" And there "was." His invitation is repeated silently, daily, hourly, with each breath. Let there be *light*…and *life*…and *Kim*…and *you*, who read this page. His ongoing invitation for us to "come" brings us back to his table again and again.

If it is Halloween, there are e-vites in my in-box. If it is the third week of the month, there are paper invitations in my mailbox. If I am still, there is a silent invitation in my soul. I try to respond yes to all the invitations, grateful to belong to something and to Someone greater than myself.

# REED AND DIANNE'S CABBAGE SLAW

*1/3 cup crushed almonds*
*1/2 head regular cabbage*
*1/2 head purple cabbage*
*2 carrots*
*1 scallion*

Preheat oven to 350 degrees. Roast almonds 10–15 minutes or until lightly brown, then set aside. Cut scallion into 1/2-inch pieces. Shred cabbage and carrots into large bowl and add scallions.

## Dressing

*1/2 cup rice vinegar, unseasoned*
*5 tablespoons granulated sugar*
*1/2 teaspoon salt*
*1/2 teaspoon dark sesame oil*
*1/4 teaspoon crushed red pepper*
*1 1/2 teaspoon fresh minced ginger*
*1 teaspoon fresh lemon juice*

Whisk together ingredients until sugar is dissolved. Add dressing to cabbage mixture and toss well to coat. Sprinkle with roasted almonds.

## CELIA'S POPPY-SEED CHICKEN

*4 boneless, skinless chicken breasts*
*1 stalk celery, whole*
*1 small onion, whole*
*1 clove garlic, whole*
*1 package chicken-flavored rice*
*1 cup sour cream*
*1 (10-ounce) can cream of chicken soup*
*1/2 teaspoon curry (optional)*
*1 tablespoon poppy seeds*
*3 tablespoons butter*
*1 cup Ritz Crackers (or other butter-flavored crackers),*
  *crumbled*

Combine chicken, celery, onion, and garlic in large pot. Cover with water. Bring to boil, then reduce heat. Simmer 20–30 minutes, or until chicken is tender. Remove chicken from pot to cool, discard vegetables, and reserve broth. In same pot, cook rice according to package directions, substituting reserved broth for water.

Preheat oven to 350 degrees. Chop chicken into bite-sized pieces and return to pot with rice. Combine remaining ingredients, except butter and crackers. Pour mixture into 9 x 13 inch casserole dish. Melt butter and mix with crackers. Sprinkle on top of casserole. Bake 30–40 minutes.

## LAURI'S BERRY BROWNIE TORTE

*3/4 cup granulated sugar*
*6 tablespoons butter*
*1 tablespoon water*
*1 1/2 cups (9 ounces) chocolate chips, divided*
*1/2 teaspoon vanilla extract*
*2 large eggs*
*2/3 cup all-purpose flour*
*1/4 teaspoon baking soda*
*1/4 teaspoon salt*

Preheat oven to 350 degrees. Grease a round 9-inch cake pan and line with parchment. Combine sugar, butter, and water in medium saucepan. Bring to a boil, stirring constantly. Remove from heat. Add 3/4 cup chocolate chips and stir until smooth. Stir in vanilla. Add eggs, one at a time, stirring well after each is added. Add flour, baking soda, and salt. Stir until well blended. Stir in remaining 3/4 cup chips. Pour into pan and bake 20–25 minutes. Cool 15 minutes in pan, then invert cake onto rack and remove parchment. Turn right-side up to cool completely.

### Filling
*1/2 cup heavy whipping cream*
*1/4 cup granulated sugar*

Beat whipping cream and sugar in small bowl until stiff peaks form.

### Garnish

   2 cups sliced strawberries and blueberries (or other fruit)

### Topping Sauce

   1/2 cup chocolate chips
   2 tablespoons light corn syrup
   1 tablespoon butter

Melt chocolate chips, corn syrup, and butter in small saucepan over low heat until smooth.

   Spread filling over brownie, then distribute fruit over top of brownie. Drizzle with chocolate sauce. Refrigerate before serving.

# TASTE AND SEE

## *The Risk of Taking a Plate*

Cherries are in season. Jim just bought four pounds at the grocery store. I was both relieved and disappointed at how few cherries equal four pounds. I was relieved because the two of us are not usually able to eat all the fruit we buy, and I would hate to have to throw away uneaten cherries. I was disappointed because I eat them like candy, and I expected four pounds of cherries to be a nearly bottomless supply.

The burgundy baubles would make a lovely beaded necklace, I imagine, but I opt for eating them instead. In the afternoon I like to put a handful in a bowl and let them warm to room temperature from their refrigerated state. Then I select them one at a time and pull the flesh from the stem with my front teeth. I drop the stems and spit the pits into the bowl and reach for another cherry with my juice-stained fingers. I usually eat too many and get a stomachache.

What of the remnants of things eaten? Pits tell the story

of once-ripe fruit, chosen and eaten, likely enjoyed. At the potluck, we throw away plates that have all kinds of stories to tell—stories of food selected, tried, and enjoyed, and other food selected, tried, and rejected.

Some of the plates we pile into the large black trash bags are slick, clean, clear of hints as to what they once contained. This indicates someone with a robust appetite who enjoyed everything, or, conversely, someone with a finicky appetite who selected little, if anything, and only something sure to be liked. My personal favorite is a plate with a small pile of leftovers that is tossed into the trash. It is testimony to an adventurous eater who was willing to select many things, to try something before rejecting it.

The nature of the potluck beckons even the pickiest of eaters to seek and find, forage and dine. I suppose that is why the plates left unused are the ones that baffle me most. They are the plates of the reluctant diners. How is it that with so much, some still leave having found nothing to eat?

A reluctant diner is a challenge for any host. If I see someone leave the table without serving up any food, I feel I have somehow let her down. Could I do more to encourage her to eat? Could I have set the table in a more inviting way? How do we encourage the reluctant diner to pick up a spoon and serve himself, to go beyond the appearance of a dish? Some people refuse to try something simply because it looks unfamiliar. On the other hand, sometimes they refuse to taste because it *is* familiar. Can you undo years of food prejudice with one trip to the table?

My own food history causes me to resist brussels sprouts to this day. I remember being urged to "clean my plate" one evening at the family dinner table. That long night ended with warm milk chasing down cold brussels sprouts. If I, a willing diner comfortable at the potluck table, have a resistance to certain foods, new or reluctant diners must surely have memories that hinder them from serving up a full plate. When I told my friend Cindi about my childhood experience with brussels sprouts, she instantly went into the merits and joys of the tiny orblike vegetable and encouraged me to give them another try. Personal testimony is a most powerful persuasion, and I just might consider steaming, grilling, frying, or poaching a few of the little cabbages again.

This past winter we had some reluctant diners at the Village Chapel potluck. It was their first time to visit with us, and they were unprepared for the dinner that followed the service. We invited them to stay and be our guests—we had plenty to share. I watched them linger behind the crowd but resist entering in. They never took a plate, never served themselves any food. I haven't seen them since, and I worry that they left hungry, unsatisfied. I wonder what we could have done to make them more comfortable, more welcome. How might we have been able to persuade them to try the food, to find something satisfying? Perhaps they were uncomfortable taking something because they didn't bring anything. But the great thing about the potluck is that it is graceful. Bringers bring extra so that those who come with nothing can still be invited. There are mysteries and complexities behind the faces of those who come through our doors, and I suppose that even a broad welcome isn't enough to urge some diners. The host in me finds it difficult to accept that sometimes it is not that the potluck has been tried and found wanting, but that it has simply been left untried.

Reluctant diners are complex. They may come to the table with broken or fearful palates, fading or stolen appetites, bad memories or biases that will take time to unravel. I hope people will find a place at our potlucks where they can tend and mend their wounded appetites. I hope we will give a warm and easy welcome, offer a wide selection, gently invite the diner to taste and see. But at some point, the wary diner will have to take the vulnerable step of approaching the table, taking a plate, and serving herself—if not at our potluck, maybe at the table at Christ Church Cathedral downtown, or First Presbyterian, or Redeemer, or Grace Community. There is a place for everyone. The table is big.

# Cindi's Grilled Brussels Sprouts
## and Cauliflower

*1 pound brussels sprouts, washed and trimmed*
*1 pound cauliflower, washed and trimmed*
*1 garlic clove, chopped*
*2 tablespoons olive oil*
*2 sprigs rosemary*
*1 tablespoon cumin seeds*
*pepper, to taste*
*basmati rice*
*lemon juice*

Cut brussels sprouts in half. Brush sprouts, cauliflower, and garlic with olive oil. Place in large bowl with rosemary, cumin seeds, and pepper. Mix thoroughly. Thread vegetables onto skewers. Grill 3–5 minutes, until vegetables are soft. Place skewers over cooked basmati rice. Sprinkle with lemon juice and serve.

*Note:* Instead of grilling vegetables, try roasting them in a 450-degree oven for 10 minutes.

# OPEN-HOUSE POTLUCK

## *Being Grafted In*

The tables in the dining room and on the back porch were covered with unmatched serving dishes from homes across Nashville. The nice thing about an open-house potluck is that late-arriving food is easily grafted in to the potluck table. Entrées, desserts, and appetizers sit in a random arrangement that makes perfect sense in this context, regardless of when they appeared.

This particular open-house potluck was in honor of a new member of Deb and Steve's family. After a long year of bureaucratic details, Sarah was finally here.

Deb and I have been friends for almost twenty years. From the time we met, people have assumed we are sisters. This is ironic, since she is a blonde and I am a brunette, her hair is short and mine is long. Complete strangers who worked in stores we had both been to, but not together, would confuse the two of us, calling us by each other's names. I recently went to a new person to have my hair cut. So did

Deb, but neither of us knew about our respective changes. Today at lunch Deb told me that at her first visit to the new stylist, the girl said, "You remind me of a woman whose hair I cut last week. Her name is Kim Thomas." She didn't know either of us or that we knew each other.

Deb and I actually met in the first place because the daughter of a mutual acquaintance saw the shoes we wore and said we should be friends. We both wore black Kenneth Cole platform sandals, which were very unusual at that time in Nashville. At five-year-old Quinn's urging, Deb and I met and discovered that we had much more than shoes in common.

Besides our many shared instincts and interests, we enjoy our differences. Deb finds the quiet beauty in life that I am usually moving too fast to notice. She taught me to slow down and drink tea, especially from a carefully collected set of unmatched teacups. When I admired her antique dessert plates, she showed up at my house with a set of six, wrapped in a linen napkin and tied with a ribbon. She was painting long before I did, and when I started on my own artistic pursuit, she gave me a brush holder to put wet brushes in. It was to make the process of painting more special and to honor my beginnings. She is a woman of detail who hears the distinction in the songs of birds and sees the variations in the veins of leaves.

In our midforties, Deb and I had made peace with the state of nonmotherhood. It wasn't necessarily a strategic state; it was just the state we found ourselves in after the adventurous travel and busy pursuits of our thirties. We enjoyed our friends' children as well as family nieces and nephews, but our own homes remained occupied only by adults.

Deb was grateful for her life, and the particularities of it, but she had a growing restlessness that increased like labor pains. The undefined longing sent her searching. Then she was invited to participate in a trip to Africa sponsored by Compassion International, a faith-based child-advocacy organization. That trip would help Deb name her restlessness and would put her on a path to satisfying it.

Moved by the poverty and orphaned condition of many of the people she met on the trip, Deb came home animated with a growing love for a faraway people. She began a quiet study of the continent, memorizing the countries and significant information about various regions. She studied the language, practicing in the privacy of her laundry room as she repeated the words spoken on tape, piecing together the strange syllables and sounds, simple greetings and phrases— the tools of communication to be used with a forgotten people. And, especially, with one forgotten child.

On one of their return trips to Uganda, Deb and her husband, Steve, would find their hearts given to a young girl named Sarah. When they first saw her, she was with a group of children in school. School was a dirt area under a tree, and on this day the assembled students gathered in the rain to sing a song of welcome for the pale guests who had traveled so far. After the song, Deb and Steve spent time with this one young orphan, holding her small chocolate-brown hand in their milk-colored palms. Sarah's quiet demeanor and the way she huddled close to Deb's side all afternoon established an unspoken connection, a small seed of love that would grow to become the love between a mother and daughter.

Deb and Steve had the quiet, well-defined life of creative artists. Her painting and his movie making required hours of solitude and focus to inspire the astoundingly beautiful results they contribute to the arts. Their "potluck table" had already been set, established by years of chosen routine. The place settings were for two, the cups and dishes, the forks and spoons familiar and comfortable. But when they met Sarah, they decided to add a leaf to their table, pull out another place setting, and invite the little diner into their hearts. Like at our open-house potluck, the late arrival was welcome.

So they worked behind the scenes for more than a year, researching the possibilities of adopting Sarah. Every Ugandan policy was against them, yet they found favor with influencers and generous people, who helped their cause. Hours of paperwork, phone calls, and trips to Washington DC for unpredictable meetings took over their days, and Deb's paintbrushes remained dry.

Finally, they made another trip to Africa, with no return date on their tickets. A Ugandan court hearing was on the calendar, but it offered no guarantees of how the judge would rule on their request for guardianship of Sarah. They had limited e-mail access and almost no cell-phone coverage, so we savored any communication they could send. After almost two months, an e-mail came to my in-box: "Kim, we'll be coming home soon. Could you tell my parents they have a granddaughter?"

Standing by the backyard gate a few days before our potluck, I had my first glance of the two of them together. Eight-year-old Sarah's midnight-colored braids were in stark contrast to Deb's wispy blond hair. But I could not help but see a familial resemblance. I saw they both had long legs and slender hips. I noticed two heart-shaped faces that ended in delicately defined chins and elegant necks on confidently squared shoulders. As I looked at Sarah wearing her pink tennis shoes, I felt drawn to her. I knew that we would become friends, because Deb and I were friends.

The tiny stranger seemed at home, playing T-ball as if she had always played it in Uganda. Her smile stretched her lips to the edge of her dimples, and her communal sense of living inspired the way she addressed the women she began to meet: "Mamma-Miró," "Mamma-Brette," "Mamma-Oliver," connecting the "Mammas" with their children. I was a bit of a problem for her because I had no children, but that didn't stop her from identifying me as "My Friend!" the next time we saw each other.

I sat on the porch looking out across the crowd of adults and children, Mammas and non-Mammas who had come to welcome Sarah at the open-house potluck. Sarah was playing with Miró, the baby girl we had celebrated at the cake-potluck baby shower twelve years earlier. Miró was wearing the sarong Sarah had given her, and Sarah was carrying the baby doll Miró had given her. Their white and dark skins were pages from the same book, young women who would grow into old women. They would be mothered and loved in their families, and I would relish the role of "Auntie" and "Friend."

The paintbrushes are wet again at Deb's house, but a different artist is in residence. Sarah painted a picture of Deb, Steve, and herself, and she painted the words *Mamma-Sarah* on the paper.

Deb worries, as we all do in our own lives, whether she is doing the right thing at the right time. Mothering instincts and wisdom will come in time. For now, she is doing what she does so well, introducing Sarah to the simple beauty of life. As for Sarah, she is pleased to finally have a "Mamma" to go with "Sarah."

The other day Deb and I met at Las Paletas, a Mexican popsicle store near our homes, while Sarah was spending time with Steve. We sat on a bench, licking our popsicles and catching up. We were both still wearing black sandals, but not so much the same. Time has taken us on different paths, and we have needed different shoes for our respective journeys. But we still belong to each other; our titles or pursuits cannot separate us. We always find our way back to the table together for popsicles, potlucks, or tea in carefully collected unmatched teacups.

## SARAH'S FAVORITE UGANDAN CHICKEN

*1 large frying chicken*
*1–2 tablespoons olive oil*
*1 large white or yellow onion, chopped*
*8 fresh tomatoes, chopped*
*salt, to taste*
*2 garlic cloves, minced*
*water*

Cut chicken into pieces, as desired. In large skillet, brown chicken in oil. Add onion and stir until onion is tender. Add tomatoes and salt. Stir until tomatoes are mashed, then add garlic. Cover chicken with water. (If you prefer less juice, add less water.) Cover and simmer about 1 hour or until chicken is tender.

# EVY'S MOROCCAN STEW

*1 pound cubed beef, lamb, or chicken*

*2 large white or yellow onions, chopped*

*1 green pepper, chopped*

*1 teaspoon ginger*

*1/4 teaspoon turmeric*

*1/4 teaspoon ground cinnamon*

*1 pinch saffron*

*2 diced carrots*

*3 chopped tomatoes, or 1 small can stewed tomatoes*

*1 pound squash, cubed*

*1 cup raisins*

*1 (20-ounce) can chickpeas, undrained*

*salt and pepper, to taste*

*cooked couscous, to serve*

Place first 10 ingredients in a large pot and cover with water. Cover and bring to a boil. Reduce heat and simmer 1 hour. Add raisins, chickpeas, salt, and pepper. Simmer another 30 minutes. Serve over couscous.

# DOWNTOWN POTLUCK

*Serving Rather than Being Served*

Our nondenominational church will join with downtown First Baptist again this winter to help fulfill the vision God gave a Catholic priest named Father Charles Strobel more than twenty years ago. Room in the Inn is potluck at its finest. Through the gifts and time of volunteers, the program provides the homeless with dinner, a warm and safe place to sleep, breakfast, a sack lunch to go, and laundered clothes each night of the week at different churches across Nashville. On Sunday nights, First Baptist is the host, welcoming thirty unknown faces during the coldest months of the year. The gymnasium is transformed into a refuge, and we come together at a table where we are privileged to serve.

Most of the people who come through the door are newly homeless. They all have stories and names and disappointments that have pooled them together in this unexpected demographic. Sometimes it feels as if we are placing a

Band-Aid on hemorrhaging wounds. But at least for this night, our guests sleep safely, and with full stomachs.

In early December the Village Chapel takes over the responsibilities so that our friends in the downtown church can celebrate their Christmas program. The other Sunday that we volunteer to serve is Super Bowl Sunday, which falls in late January or early February. So on one Sunday night, someone will be singing "Joy to the World," and on another someone will be watching a field goal being kicked.

Scott organizes the overnight effort at the Village Chapel. He lives four houses down the street from Jim and me in the cul-de-sac. Forty-something and single, he bought and reno-vated his 1920s home about five years ago. He is a member of the Servant Leadership Council for the Village Chapel, and he is also a good friend. If I am ever out of town, he takes Jim out for steak. If Jim is ever out of town, Scott is on my speed dial, in case of emergency. He is a good man, and I am con-stantly trying to marry him off to someone. I feel certain that is annoying to him, and so I'm trying to knock it off.

Many years ago Scott was in the restaurant business. We benefit from this latent love of his. When he doesn't bring his homemade fried chicken or barbecued ribs to our potlucks, he whips up a pot of tortilla soup or his world-famous tossed salad with the secret olive-oil-and-something dressing. At our summer outdoor potlucks, Scott is typically slaving over the grill, usually a grill he loaded into the back of his GMC and brought with him. Generosity is who Scott is.

On Room in the Inn Sundays, Scott rallies the volunteers to care for the thirty overnight guests. We need people to drive the vans from the rescue mission to the church, make sack lunches, cook dinner, set up beds in the gymnasium, mingle and share with the guests, wash the guests' clothes, provide overnight security, prepare breakfast, take down the bedding, and then drive the guests back to the mission for early morning work pickup. Scott mingles with people after Sunday church weeks before our turn at the inn, carrying a sign-up clipboard. Little cajoling is necessary. People are always looking for Scott, anxious to put their names down on the volunteer list.

Super Bowl Sunday is a particularly eventful night at Room in the Inn. Not only does Scott gather the volunteers for the normal tasks; he also sets about making a party out of the evening. Rather than hauling a grill, his GMC carts a big-screen TV for watching the game. Scott also finds time to prepare chicken wings, trays of shrimp cocktail, and other football food for guests to munch on before dinner. Several from our group provide the actual dinner, like Janice who makes a chicken pot pie or Joyce who makes up a pot of Super Bowl chili. Robin packs up sack lunches of sandwiches, fruit, and chips at her house and brings them down that evening, and Tammy brings a fruit salad and stays to help serve.

So the potluck table is plentiful, a group *hungry to give* brings the food, and a group *hungry to partake* comes. Danny is a talented musician who attends the Village Chapel. He sits with two men, and they talk about football, a universal language that makes comrades of strangers. Janice, also from the Chapel, is a mother of a teenage boy. Her mother's heart is broken as she talks to a young woman who has been living in a car with her two children. Other quiet conversations are initiated throughout the room, and an unlikely community forms as each volunteer becomes an image bearer of God, sharing food on a winter night.

The guests do not expect a big-screen TV or shrimp cocktail or chicken wings. In fact, they don't expect anything. Most days their focus is on survival. But Scott wants to give them something beyond just surviving, more than the minimum. He wants to provide something memorable, a potluck welcome that might warm more than just their hands and feet. He leads our small group in the path of serving, inviting others in from the cold. And for at least one night, he is turning water into wine, serving up the best when less would have been enough. To the glory of God.

# SCOTT'S TORTILLA SOUP

4 corn tortillas, coarsely chopped
2 1/2 tablespoons all-purpose flour
1 teaspoon chili powder
1 teaspoon salt
pepper, to taste
1 teaspoon cumin
1 tablespoon vegetable oil
1 1/2 tablespoons butter
3 tablespoons minced yellow onion
2 tablespoons seeded and minced green pepper
1 1/2 teaspoon minced fresh garlic
1 quart chicken stock
1 chicken breast, poached and cut up
cheddar cheese, grated (or other variety as desired)
tortilla chips, to serve

Place tortilla pieces, flour, chili powder, salt, pepper, and cumin
in food processor and mix until it is the consistency of cornmeal.
Set aside. Heat oil and butter in large saucepan and add onion,
green pepper, and garlic. Sauté over medium-high heat until
soft. Add tortilla mixture to sautéed vegetables and stir. The
mixture will pull away from the sides of the pan and start to
form a ball. Add chicken stock slowly, whisking out any lumps.
After stock is incorporated, bring mixture to a boil. Reduce

heat, add chicken, and simmer 15–20 minutes, stirring occasionally.

Before serving, process soup in food processor. Top with grated cheese and tortilla chips. (Makes 1 quart or 4 servings.)

# A PLATE FOR EVERYONE

*Seeing a Need and Responding*

Every Sunday evening when I walk into the old Saint Bernard building before our church service, I stop in the children's room before continuing down the hall to the chapel. The creaking floor does not allow me to make a silent entrance, and the young faces in the room are already looking up when I come in. Nate usually throws an excited question my way: "Miss Kim, Miss Kim, is Pastor Jim here?"

I don't take offense that my presence is only a means to determine someone else's. I am happy to be greeted by name and with such enthusiasm. Nate is at an age when "guys" are his preferred people, and though my instinct is to cuddle him, touch his summer-blond head, and gently pat his back, these are not his favorite forms of connection. So we talk about the cartoon characters he likes to draw and discuss Thomas the Tank Engine. By then he is pretty much done with me, and if Pastor Jim is not coming, Nate asks, "How about James Gregory?"

Nate is the son of Mike and Nancy. They live a few blocks from us and have been Nashvillians longer than most people I know. We became friends when they started coming to the Village Chapel. Mike is a freelance writer, who works on projects from books and movies to tire campaigns and TV scripts. Nancy is a college instructor and an educational consultant, and we discovered during our first lunch together at El Palenque that we have the same devious sense of humor. We have on more than one occasion contemplated hosting our own TV show: *The Nancy and Kim Comedy Hour That No One but Nancy and Kim Will Laugh at Because No One Else Has a Very Good Sense of Humor.* We are quite hilarious and entertain ourselves effortlessly.

Mike, Nancy, and Nate are always at the building before I get there on Sundays. They have volunteered to be the setup team for the nursery every week. This entails coming early enough to load the elevator three times with rockers, bookcases, changing tables, toys, and general nursery supplies, and take it all up to the next floor, unload it, and set up our movable nursery.

Since Nate is eight years old now, Mike and Nancy have no babies of their own in the nursery, but they saw a need and filled it. Fortunately, the nursery setup coincides with Nate's eagerness to come to the Village Chapel. Mike and Nancy tell me that Nate wakes up on Sunday mornings and asks, "Is it time to go to the Village Chapel yet?"

Mike and Nancy explain to him, "No, not until later today, Nate." And when he asks again in ten minutes, they say, "Not yet, Nate. Just a little longer."

Coming early seems to be a good thing for them. I know it is a good thing for us.

Mike and Nancy don't get hung up on analyzing whether they feel they are "called" to answer the need or whether it is an appropriate match for their "gifting." They see a need, and as far as it is within their power to meet it, they do. I remember that when we reprinted the church directory, Mike called Jim and said, "I've been looking at the addresses, and I see nine or ten on our side of Hillsboro Road. Okay if we have a dinner and invite people over to get to know each other?"

Jim smiled and said, "That would be great, Mike."

Over the years I have been the happy recipient of this family's generous food gifting. When Jim and I were home alone for Thanksgiving because I was sick, peanut-butter pie, rolls, and sweet-potato casserole were delivered in a Red Riding Hood–sized basket to our front door. Mike said, "Our upbringing has irrevocably affected us, and when there is sickness, we instinctively respond with food."

Actually, sickness, sadness, deadlines, or celebrations call them into action. Nate, Mike, and Nancy are a family team, and they each find a place at their kitchen counter for making something to give away. At the first few potlucks we had at the Village Chapel, they brought a collection of casseroles, salads, and desserts. But recently I saw them come in carrying a large platter piled with little, crustless white-bread sandwiches in cookie-cutter shapes. They had overheard the kids complaining at potlucks that there was nothing good to eat.

Most of us see the opportunity to prepare a potluck dish as a culinary challenge, and out come the Asian, Indian, Mexican, Italian, French, and Moroccan recipes. The macaroni-and-cheese staples of days gone by are in danger of extinction, and evidently the children will starve if something doesn't change. So Mike and Nancy once again saw a need and responded. They decided to love children at potlucks and prepare peanut-butter-and-jelly sandwiches on white bread, cut out with cookie cutters. That night we had star-shaped, gingerbread man–shaped, heart-shaped, and tree-shaped PB&J sandwiches that nearly leaped off the serving platter into eager little hands. The children's faces turned from uncertain to jubilant as they loaded their Styrofoam plates with staples of their childhood diet.

The potluck table is meant to offer something for everyone. Just when the table might seem overwhelming and unfamiliar to some of our diners, a plate of simple peanut-butter-and-jelly sandwiches shows up. Mike and Nancy remind me to keep the welcome simple, straightforward, and on a plate that everyone can reach.

# NANCY, MIKE, AND NATE'S PB&J SANDWICHES

1. Start with a loaf of extra-thin Pepperidge Farm bread—wheat if you can get away with it; white if you're dealing with purists.

2. Lay out the pieces on the counter and spread half of them with a thin layer of creamy peanut butter.

3. Spread the remaining pieces with a thin layer of strawberry jam if you can get away with it; grape jelly if you're dealing with purists. *Note:* If you spread the peanut butter or jam too thick, your shapes will become unrecognizable blobs. In this case, thin is in.

4. Match peanut buttered halves with jellied halves to assemble sandwiches.

5. Using gingerbread man–shaped, heart-shaped, bunny-shaped, or other favorite-shaped cookie cutters, carefully cut shapes from the centers of the sandwiches. *Note:* Some smaller shapes will allow for two shapes per sandwich, but you must be extra careful to be sure the shapes do not include crust.

6. Festively arrange the sandwich shapes on plates for the kids. Display with an appropriate love note, such as "Somebunny-loves-you PB&Js."

7. Slap the remaining scraps and crusts on a plate and display with the label: "Daddy Food." The daddies will dutifully consume these remains, especially if you're at a potluck that leans toward organic/vegetarian dishes.

# A BASKET OF SOUL FOOD

### *"Enough" Is Always Satisfying*

I am always surprised at the randomly organized arrival of "enough" at our potlucks. We do not give strict dish assignments to people, such as requesting entrées from those with last names beginning with "A–G," salads "H–M," and so on. Our group has never been much for overorganization. And even though the potential success or failure of our potlucks stresses me, I have seen that in response to a simple invitation to bring *something*, each person does his or her part, and enough arrives for all.

"Enough" is sometimes accomplished with one person's jam served on another's bread, since most dishes brought to the potluck do not constitute a meal on their own. Last summer, for instance, Wendy Lee brought a basket of homemade popovers. (*Lee* is not Wendy Lee's last name, and she is not simply "Wendy;" she is "Wendy Lee.") She used to eat the hollow little milk-flour-and-egg muffins at Macy's Café. When the café closed, she figured out how to make them herself and now shares that goodness with us. Popovers and honey-butter alone would (debatably) not make a meal. But at our potluck, they were transformed into something greater than themselves by their relationship to the casseroles and salads beside them. In the collective spread, they became enough.

Wendy Lee is a writer and mines her mental storehouse of words most days. We both eat out frequently, and since we have similar writing schedules, we find time for lunch together every couple of weeks. Her under-forty-and-single view of life brings a different perspective to our table than my over-forty-and-married one. We talk about the things unique to our own passages in life and the things that we have in common as women, writers, and friends. This sisterhood is usually shared at a Caribbean restaurant over slow-roasted chicken, black beans, and mustard greens.

She has been a missionary to Amsterdam, an intern at a young women's magazine in New York City, a preschool teacher, the editor of a women's magazine in Nashville, and she has written a shelf full of books. In her twenties she picked up and moved across the country and the globe several times. Then, after years of living in temporary dwellings, she bought a house in Nashville last year, finally making a permanent home here.

Wendy Lee does not sit and wait for life to happen. She intentionally pursues it. She is a professional and good at what she does, but professional pursuits and income earning have never been so consuming that she didn't make time for the people she is in heart-proximity to. I see Wendy Lee as a woman who understands what makes life rich and chooses it. Her connection to her family and friends is the core thread that supports her life structure, and she diligently builds on that. Somewhere between want and too much is the loveliness of "enough." That's where Wendy Lee lives. It's not that she settles for less but that she finds the abundance of contentment in giving herself away.

On Sunday nights Wendy Lee is always willing to braid eleven-year-old Isabella's hair at the pizza place we all go to after church. I hear about how she baby-sat for the children of a couple who rarely have time alone, or how she went to help someone make kitchen curtains. I know about her driving to meet a new mom for a rare lunch outing, and how she gave up an evening recently to teach a group of young women how to knit. And I was there when she came to Isaiah's last Little League game of the summer. She made me a card when I started writing this book, reminding me that good work is always worth the extra effort and that there will be those who will see and appreciate it. In words that only a fellow writer would think to use, she urged me to be generous with my soul.

Wendy Lee shows up in her overalls when there is hard work to be done, and in her green-flowered spring jacket when there is simply time to be shared. She directed the volunteers at our church workday that benefits a local afterschool program. Tireless in the summer heat, she coordinated the repair of a playground as well as the ground-up construction of a rock-climbing wall, not because she knows how to fix playgrounds or do construction, but because she gives what she has, and it becomes enough.

With all Wendy Lee gives, I often worry that there will be nothing left for her at the end of a day, and I want to guard her portion of enough. But I am reminded of a story about a young boy who gave all he had and how it became enough.

At a gathering on a Middle Eastern hill in the region of Bethsaida Julius, a crowd had assembled to listen to the Master. At the end of the day, the hosts in charge were concerned about how they were going to feed the impromptu crowd of more than five thousand. A young boy came forward with his small lunchbox. Undaunted by the numbers that didn't add up, he simply brought his small potluck offering of five loaves and two fishes. The Master blessed the food and directed the hosts to distribute it to the waiting and hungry crowd. Through no sleight of hand or tricks, and with extremely little organization, a basket of five loaves and two fishes became enough. Even more astounding, after feeding the entire group to total satisfaction, the twelve hungry servants collected the leftovers. There were exactly twelve baskets of leftovers. It would have been "too much" if there had been fifteen, "too little" if there had been ten, but twelve—that was "enough" for the twelve servants. When we give ourselves away, the Master makes sure there is always enough left over for us.

Wendy Lee's basket was empty when she took it home the night of our potluck. I picture her walking to the parking lot after she had, of course, stayed to help clean up, and I see her smiling. What Wendy Lee gives is not pretentious or conspicuous, but it is willing and generous. The God of all abundance makes it a glorious enough. I have a feeling that pleases her, and perhaps that was exactly what was leftover in her basket: a soul full of satisfaction.

# WENDY LEE'S POPOVERS

*1 cup milk*
*1 cup all-purpose flour*
*3 eggs*
*2 teaspoons vegetable oil*
*1/2 teaspoon salt*

Preheat oven to 450 degrees. Place greased popover tin or large muffin tin in oven to preheat. Combine all ingredients in blender on high speed until bubbles form (about 10 seconds). Fill each section of popover or muffin tin 1/2 to 3/4 full. Place tin in oven at once. Reduce heat to 425 degrees and bake 20 minutes. Reduce heat again to 350 degrees and bake an additional 20 minutes. Serve immediately.

# PREWEDDING POTLUCK

*Mingling Our Salt*

Peter and Whitney are getting married tomorrow. They started coming to the Village Chapel a couple of years ago and met in the company of our eclectic and warm group of twenty-somethings. Just before sunset they will be married at Saddlebrook Farm on a green hill. Jim will wear a suit and perform the honorable role of pastor, directing them as they promise their love and lives to each other.

The bride is a tall young woman whose frail exterior gives no hint of the strong interior that sturdies her in life. Thin as a whisper and carefully spoken, Whitney is graceful in spirit, creative, and thoughtful. She is the oldest of three sisters, with whom she fought over who got the biggest room, the last piece of pizza, clothes, bathroom time, keys to the family car, or Mom and Dad's affections. These same bickering sisters, who have become young women, will stand by Whitney as bridesmaids. They will smile and cry and be proud of her.

From the first Sunday Whitney visited with us, I wanted to make a comfortable place for her. I was so pleased when a lovely couple in the church offered her a place to live just blocks from the church, and she became a youthful fixture at our gatherings. With a degree in art education, she was on a hunt for the career that would maximize her talents and desires. She moved to Nashville from Georgia for various reasons, and whether in spite of or because of those reasons, she found a place of belonging here. Over soup at a local Chinese restaurant one night, we talked about things of substance that were resonating with her, and other things that troubled her and weighed on her delicate shoulders. Time has passed so quickly since that night. Now Whitney is marrying Peter.

I knew the groom as the young man who sat in the back of the room for a long time. Most obviously distinguished by black-rimmed glasses that gave him a wide-eyed, hip-geek presence, I noticed that he quietly continued to show up at the Chapel. At first it was Sundays, then Wednesdays too. Then he was volunteering to help do whatever needed to be done. It was clear that he had begun to grow roots in our little community.

Peter drives a half hour on Tuesday mornings to be part of our men's group that meets at 8:00 at Puckett's Grocery, which is a telling sign of commitment for anyone. Personally, I am most committed to gatherings after 10:00 a.m. As he pursues character and personal integrity, the good man Peter is becoming distinguishes him now far more than his glasses.

He is a talented musician and a trained engineer who found his way to Nashville from Minnesota. So north and south converged in a little church in Hillsboro Village. Now Peter is marrying Whitney.

We'll all make our way to Saddlebrook Farm for the wedding, the twenty-five-acre home of Matt and Kristin and their two sons, Harrison and Sam. They have worked hard for the past month to prepare the farm for the convergence of wedding guests. The wedding will christen their land for what they always intended it to be, a gathering place for community. Those who come as witnesses to Peter and Whitney's vows will drive over a long gravel road, walk up a gradual slope, and sit in white chairs on that green hill of Saddlebrook Farm.

Tonight Peter and Whitney's friends are throwing them a prewedding Potluck in the Park. The muggy evening in Sevier Park is transformed by red lanterns and balloons, tablecloths on picnic tables, towering vases of Asian flowers in spare bloom, and a table full of fresh summer food brought by friends and family. I put a little of Janice's Curried-Chicken-and-Rice Salad and Kristin's Cranberry-Nut Salad on my red paper plate and follow that up with generous helpings of ripe cantaloupe and plump green grapes. Then I fill a clear plastic cup with pink lemonade and enjoy conversation with Dan and June, Nancy, Carla, and Janice at the last picnic table under the pavilion.

The relatives of the bride and groom mingle with typical

awkwardness, getting to know the different family rhythms. By evening's end, it seems the merging of the families has successfully begun, and aunts, uncles, grandparents, cousins, and children become one large extended family. Not only are the bride and groom choosing each other, but the families choose each other too. I meet the occasional uncle or distant cousin and an old roommate of the bride or groom, and I watch as Whitney's grandmom stares at her with pride. When we say good-bye for the evening, I hug this lovely matriarch. Her skin is soft and thin as paper, and she smells like the sachets you put in your lingerie drawer. We agree to have lunch when she comes back to town, and I promise to keep a watchful eye on her granddaughter. We all fight off the fierce mosquitoes, and when a summer rain moves in to consume the evening, everyone dashes to their cars in the gravel parking lot.

My wet legs stick to the leather seat as Jim and I drive the seven blocks to our house. The smell of bug spray and sweat permeates the car, and the heat and humidity steam up the windows. I reach up and scrawl "Peter loves Whitney" on the window with my finger.

In their ceremony, Peter and Whitney will celebrate the Covenant of Salt. It is an ancient tradition in which two parties gave each other their word and, to seal their commitment, brought salt from their respective homes and poured it into a neutral container. The vow could only be broken if one of the two parties was able to remove all the grains of salt he or she had brought from home that had mingled with the grains the other party had brought.

At tonight's potluck, in a similar act of intention, the families and friends of the bride and groom mingled their salt. That is the intention of all of our potlucks, that our salt would mingle and our commitment to one another would become a covenant of faithfulness.

The bride and groom will bring the best of who they are to the sacramental table of marriage and offer it to each other. Then they will publicly covenant to take each other, hold each other, care for each other, grow old with each other. Jim will lead them in their vows, we will all try not to cry, and Jim will say, "I now pronounce you…" Peter will take Whitney's face in his hands, their eyes will be moist, and he will kiss her lips. They will lean against each other for strength in the warm evening before they turn to face the people gathered to bear witness to their love on the green hill. It will be the first of many leanings, the millions that will make up the days of their marriage. Then they will turn and smile and hold each other's hands as they walk past all of us back down the green hill of Saddlebrook Farm.

Then we will *all* eat cake.

## JANICE'S CURRIED-CHICKEN-AND-RICE SALAD

1 1/4 cups mayonnaise

1 1/2 teaspoons curry powder

2 cups cooked rice

2 boneless, skinless chicken breasts, cooked and diced

1/3 cup chopped green onion

1 1/2 teaspoons lemon juice

1 1/2 cups cooked green peas

2 tablespoons diced pimento

1 cup chopped celery

salt and pepper, to taste

Combine all ingredients. Season to taste with salt and pepper.

## KRISTIN'S CRANBERRY-NUT SALAD

*1 bunch romaine lettuce, washed and torn*
*1/2 cup sunflower seeds (unsalted work best)*
*1/2 cup shredded, fresh parmesan cheese*
*1/2 cup dried cranberries*
*Newman's Own Balsamic Vinaigrette dressing, to taste*

Toss first 4 ingredients in large bowl. Add salad dressing to taste and toss.

# NOTES IN THE MARGINS

*Recording the Stories of Life*

When Jim and I wanted my dad's permission to get married twenty-eight years ago and Dad was hesitant, we jokingly asked him if he needed a 3 x 5 card from God on the subject. Without missing a breath he said, "Yes, that would be fine."

My dad almost always carries 3 x 5 cards in his shirt pocket. They were the original PDA for him, reminding him of things to do, phone numbers he needed to remember, ticklers for long-range goals. We sometimes jest that if it isn't on a 3 x 5 card, Dad isn't going to do it.

A year after Jim and I asked permission to be married, it seemed that God sent a 3 x 5 card to Dad. He retired from the navy and took a job in another state. Perhaps time and God's curious arrangement of circumstances combined to persuade Dad to consent, but we all like to think of it as Dad's 3 x 5 from God. With joy and confidence, he and Mom consented to Jim and I marrying.

In the many years since then, I have, ironically, found myself using 3 x 5 cards to help order parts of my own life. I keep some by my bed, in my purse, in the kitchen, and in the car. They are perfect, stout cards for making notes, listing reminders of things to do, and recording things of interest or significance as they come across my path.

This morning Dad sent me a 3 x 5 card from Mom's recipe box. It was one I had asked him to look for, and he was so pleased to have found it for me. The recipe itself was actually irrelevant at that point, but the card held value beyond its original intent.

Mom's handwriting filled one side of the recipe card. It was a list of ingredients and instructions, as well as some suggestions for alternate ingredients. I touched it with my fingertips and held it up to my cheek. The grief of losing Mom to cancer remains close to the surface.

The other side of the card was covered in spontaneous doodles—by me. I must have been preschool age, and I had written my name, misspelling it. A few letters I must have been practicing were repeated across the top, and toward the bottom of the card were two figures that looked like legless and armless people, one tall and one short. Perhaps a mommy and her daughter.

It was the most perfect 3 x 5 card I had ever held. It carried things smudged by one small hand with fat fingers and other things carefully recorded by long graceful fingers on a womanly hand. I hadn't felt this close to Mom in a long time.

I pictured Dad looking for the card late into the night, his house stilled and inhabited by one less. I thought about the sacrifice it was for him to experience the emotions that each card in Mom's recipe box brought forth, the memories that must have assaulted him. Some of the recipes probably brought a smile to his face; some may have even made him hungry. But all of them were reminders of the soul mate who cooked them for him for fifty years. The quiet house must have been a loud reminder of her absence.

Most of the recipe cards in Mom's box are simple lists and instructions, chronicles of dishes she made for us over the years. But many of the cards have notes in the margins, personal comments about what event she made the dish for, how successful it was, or how she would do it differently next time. "Use butter instead of margarine," "Double the curry next time," "Works nicely with a spinach salad and La Sueur peas," she wrote. The comments make the cards into time capsules that had recorded the notes and stories of her life.

Now that I am a wife, I have my own 3 x 5 box full of recipes. It is a little worn for the years, and the lid broke off at least a decade ago. All the recipe cards stick out the top of the box like windblown heads in a Chevy convertible. I, too, have cards with notes scratched in the margins, such as the recipe I copied from Mom for Consommé Rice. After following the simple instructions to "brown rice in butter, add toasted almonds, consommé, and mushrooms," I served up teeth-cracking rice to my guests. I went back and made the note in the margin, "Cook for one hour at 350 degrees." In this case, the margin note became as essential as the original instructions.

Margin notes chronicle failures and successes, experiments and discoveries. Our lives have similar notes. Sometimes they are scribbled exclamations of celebration, and sometimes they are tear-smeared records of disappointment and loss. They tell our stories beyond the simple straightforward information of our names, our jobs, our demographic. These are the notes that reveal our hearts, records of what makes us who we are. They are best preserved when we share them. I suppose that's what we do at our potlucks. We pull up a chair to the table and exchange "recipes," sharing beyond the simple ingredient list of our lives and revealing the personal notes that chronicle our stories.

So this morning I held Mom's card in my hand, and I imagined the margin notes of her life, the ways she filled every moment with purpose and dignity. I was glad for how generously she shared her notes with me. And as I looked at the recipe card, I couldn't help but notice the arrow at the bottom indicating more notes on the back of the card. I smiled to myself, knowing that indeed the notes of Mom's life are "continued on the other side."

## MOM'S CONSOMMÉ RICE

*1/2 cup butter*
*1 cup uncooked rice*
*1/2 cup slivered almonds*
*small can mushrooms, drained*
*1 can beef consommé*

Preheat oven to 350 degrees. Melt butter in frying pan. Add rice and brown over medium heat. Toast almonds. Pour consommé and mushrooms into 1-quart casserole dish. Add rice and almonds. Cover and cook 1 hour.

# BROKEN BREAD

## *The Potluck Gospel*

The women on the cover of this book began as doodles on the edge of my sketch pad, resulting in the first three pieces I painted for a recent art show. I spent weeks with them, drawing, painting, and getting to know the long lean ladies holding serving dishes high in front of them. They would come to be my "Potluck Ladies: Dessert, Congealed Salad, and Casserole."

Months later I displayed them and fifteen other pieces in my show. More people asked about those paintings than about any other work I showed that year, and I told the story about the Ladies dozens of times. Almost always, the other person would recount to me her own potluck memory of family meals or church gatherings or community picnics.

In spite of all the interest and conversation, the Ladies didn't sell. Instead, they stayed a few more months with me—long enough to inspire me to write.

Standing quietly in my front room, they greeted me

everytime I came or went. They silently reminded me of the quotidian simplicity of the communal meal. Broken bread, shared stories, connected lives. In their silent picture, they delivered a homily in the metaphor of the potluck, speaking a simple message that I too often had made complicated. The Potluck Gospel is that Christ has set a generous table and invites the hungry to find a seat, to be filled, and to be found. The table is long, the dishes are varied, and the welcome is big

I've heard a story about a New York City socialite. A legend in society circles, she was the reigning diva of the entertaining world. It was said that all of her parties were exceedingly well attended, invitations eagerly sought after. Everyone wanted to be asked to her gatherings. In a magazine interview she was queried about what she thought made her such a successful hostess. She replied with no hesitation: "I greet every guest when they arrive, and I say to them 'At last, you've arrived!' welcoming them as if they are uniquely important to me. And I mean it."

That story reminded me of how much I want to be greeted that way, how much I want to find that welcome. So I've changed the way I pursue belonging. I'm going to give it away to those around me. And in the giving, I might find it for myself, too. The potluck is the place where the giving, the taking, and the belonging perfectly intersect.

Perhaps you are hungry and long to find belonging too. Pull up a chair and prepare yourself a plate. And may I say, "At last, you've arrived! Let the Potluck begin."

## DESSERT: RITZ-CRACKER PIE

*3 egg whites*
*1 cup granulated sugar*
*20 Ritz Crackers, crumbled but not crushed*
*1 cup chopped pecans*
*1 teaspoon vanilla extract*
*whipped cream, for garnish*
*mandarin oranges, for garnish*

Preheat oven to 275 degrees. Beat egg whites, adding sugar very slowly. Beat to stiff peaks. Crumble 5 crackers at a time into mixture and stir with wooden spoon. Add nuts and vanilla and stir. Fold all together. Pour into greased 9-inch pie pan. Bake 1 hour. Garnish with whipped cream and mandarin oranges.

## CONGEALED SALAD: STRAWBERRY-CRANBERRY
## DELECTABLE DELIGHT

*1 (3-ounce) package strawberry Jell-O*
*1/2 cup chopped celery*
*1/2 cup chopped pecans*
*1 can cranberry sauce*

Prepare Jell-O according to package directions. Let sit in refrigerator until beginning to set (about 30 minutes), then mix in remaining ingredients. Pour into 9 x 13 inch baking dish or Jell-O mold. Refrigerate before serving.

## CASSEROLE: ARTICHOKE TART IN WALNUT PASTRY

*Pastry*

>   1 cup walnuts
>   2 cups all-purpose flour
>   1 teaspoon salt
>   1 stick (8 tablespoons) butter
>   2 eggs

Preheat oven to 375 degrees. Process walnuts in a food processor until coarsely ground. Add flour and salt. Place pats of butter on top of dry ingredients and pulse until mixed. Add eggs and process just until mixture begins to hold together. Remove dough from processor and press into bottom and sides of 9 x 13 inch baking dish. Partially bake 10 minutes.

*Filling*

>   2 cloves garlic, minced
>   2 sticks butter
>   2 (6-ounce) jars marinated artichoke hearts, drained and
>       diced
>   2 cups light cream
>   6 large eggs
>   1 teaspoon pepper
>   salt, to taste
>   16 ounces gruyère cheese, grated

Sauté garlic in butter. Add diced artichoke hearts and set aside.
Combine cream, eggs, pepper, and salt in medium bowl.
Sprinkle grated cheese over bottom of partially baked crust.
Add artichoke mixture to cream mixture. Pour over cheese and
crust. Bake 35 minutes until golden and slightly puffy and a
toothpick inserted comes out clean.

# RECIPE INDEX

# ACKNOWLEDGMENTS

Thank you to my family—The task is made easier for a writer when she has so many family stories with which to seed a book. My dear God-given family, you are an entire seed catalog for me to pick from. I am grateful for the nurturing environment you provided for me, and the template you gave me for how to be in relationship. Yours will always be the table I am most comfortable at.

Thank you to my friends and my Village Chapel family—Living with you as "chosen family" is an honor. I am inspired by your stories and the generous ways you live them out. Thank you for allowing me to tell them.

Thank you, Don Pape—for having authentic enthusiasm for this book and my work.

Thank you to my new WaterBrook family—Dudley Delffs, Shannon Hill, and the immensely talented and visionary sales and marketing departments.

Thank you, Cindi DiMarzo—for graciously inspiring and tending my early pages. You gave me courage to undo myself and regather my words.

Thank you, Sarah Fortenberry—for always being more than my agent. Friend, believer, inspirer, are only some of the ways I refer to you.

Thank you, Jim—You are the finest man I know. I respect

you and love you far more than I can begin to express. You urge the "better" from me when there is "better" to give, and you speak life to me when I do my best. If you like what I do and who I am, I am a happy woman.

# ABOUT THE AUTHOR

KIM THOMAS is the author of *Finding Your Way Through Grief, Even God Rested, Living in the Sacred Now,* and *Simplicity.* She is also a painter, best known for her cover art for the City on a Hill CD series. She makes her home in Nashville, Tennessee, with her husband, Jim.

Be sure to visit *www.KimThomasBooks.com* to get information and products for hosting a *Potluck* book club, party, or Bible study. Or you can become a part of the online *Potluck* community, meet some of the people in the book, find new and seasonal recipes, and read more "notes in the margins." You can also view some of Kim's art or send her a note.